CRYSTALS *for* HEALING

THE COMPLETE REFERENCE GUIDE WITH REMEDIES FOR MIND, HEART & SOUL

Karen Frazier

ALTHEA
PRESS

to Tanner

CRYSTALS FOR HEALING

Contents

chapter four **CRYSTAL REMEDIES FOR MIND, HEART & SOUL** 48

chapter five CRYSTAL REMEDIES FOR OVERLAPPING AREAS 210

chapter six CRYSTAL PROFILES 244

Introduction

*U*sing crystals for spiritual, emotional, mental, and physical healing is an age-old practice dating back thousands of years. Today, crystal healing is still used in our modern world, relying on the vibrations of ancient stones as a remedy for what ails us.

As a Usui Reiki Master, energy healer, and ordained metaphysical minister, I have incorporated crystals into my healing work for years. In my healing practice, I use them to focus emotional and spiritual energy to affect positive change.

Crystals have been important in my own healing journey, as well. I work with them daily to focus my meditation, improve my connection with the spiritual and my higher self, and make adjustments when I experience mental, spiritual, or emotional blockages. For example, I've used crystals to achieve forgiveness, as well as to move through grief after the recent death of a loved one. I often work with them to stimulate inspiration and creativity and to focus my intuition.

A deep connection exists between body, mind, and spirit. Imbalance affects every aspect of life, including relationships, career, hobbies, emotions, and even physical health. I learned this the hard way as a young adult. I was out of balance because I was too cerebral, spending so much time in my mind that I neglected my body and soul. This imbalance led to illness and unhappiness, and I spent most of my twenties adrift, with numerous broken relationships, job changes, unfinished projects, and different addresses to prove it.

I was in my early thirties when everything changed. I'd just gone through the breakup of another relationship and had recently lost a job I enjoyed. In the midst of this, I developed a sore throat that persisted, no matter what I tried. I visited several doctors, each unable to treat it because they couldn't find a physical cause.

I WAS MENTALLY CLEAR, & I FELT A CONNECTION TO SPIRIT THAT HAD ESCAPED ME FOR YEARS

As the severity worsened and the duration stretched from weeks to months, I decided to try alternative therapy. I found a medical doctor who also practiced energy healing techniques.

With deep skepticism, I went to my appointment. After a consultation, the doctor had me lie supine on her treatment table with a green rock on the middle of my chest and a blue rock on the center of my throat. She cupped her hands gently on the crown of my head. I felt a rush of energy, and for reasons I couldn't understand, I burst into tears. I continued sobbing for the remainder of the treatment and all the way home in my car. I cried for the rest of the day until I went to sleep that night.

When I woke up, I felt fantastic. My throat pain was gone, and I felt more alive and enthusiastic than I had in ages. I was mentally clear, and I felt a connection to spirit that had escaped me for years. My throat pain, it turned out, didn't come from any physical source, but from a spiritual and emotional one that had to do with speaking and living my truth. By clearing the energy blockage that existed in my throat, I was able to release the spiritual and emotional pain I'd been carrying, which then caused a release of the physical pain.

That single visit was the start of a host of positive changes in my life that have led me to a place of great joy, peace, and creativity that has lasted thus far for nearly twenty years. Despite my initial skepticism, my first appointment in an energy healer's office brought me to crystals and energy healing, and it empowered me to live the life my soul wanted. That's why I'm so excited to share crystal healing with you. It's a wonderful tool for finding your own spiritual, mental, and emotional empowerment so that you, too, can lead a life that truly invigorates you and brings you joy.

1
CHAPTER

The Basics of Crystal Healing

How can a rock bring about healing? After all, crystals are just pretty stones, aren't they? While it's true that crystals are stones, each has a unique structure that imparts its own energetic properties. Healers, holy people, and shamans have known about these properties for millennia. As a result, cultures throughout history have incorporated crystals into their spiritual and healing practices, and references to and the use of these energetic objects have been found in various holy texts and at archeological sites. The use of crystals for healing continues today, and with the information you will learn in this book, you can begin putting this practice to use in your life.

It Starts with Energy

According to physicist Nikola Tesla, "If you want to find the secrets of the universe, think in terms of energy, frequency, and vibration." Energy is where the secrets of crystal healing lie.

ENERGY & VIBRATION

In 1905, Albert Einstein demonstrated the relationship between matter and energy in his special theory of relativity. Over a century later, French physicist Laurent Lellouch completed calculations verifying this important relationship on a subatomic level, showing that mass could be converted to energy. Perhaps the best real-world demonstration of this relationship is nuclear energy, which results from the conversion of matter into energy.

As Einstein and others have proved, locked within each object in the universe lies some form of energy. Cyndi Dale, in her book *The Subtle Body: An Encyclopedia of Your Energetic Anatomy,* describes swirling subtle energies underlying all of physical reality and forming the basis of all matter. You, and everything around you, Dale notes, are made up of energy. This is true of living objects, such as human beings, as well as objects that are perceived to be inanimate, such as crystals. This is where humans and crystals intersect: energy and vibration.

All energetic objects vibrate, although that vibration is typically undetectable by our five senses. Nevertheless, science shows that the vibration exists and that each object has its own unique vibrational signature. In humans, this energetic signature exists in the form of our subtle energetic bodies, which include:

CHAKRAS the energy centers in the body (explained in more detail on page 23)

MERIDIANS the energetic pathways running through the body

AURAS energy fields surrounding the human body that enable us to detect our own energy and the energy of others; they are detected by special cameras in a process known as Kirlian photography

Crystals, like our bodies, have auras and vibrations of their own, and the interaction between the energy of crystals and the energy of humans can affect our vibrations. Using crystals helps us modulate our energetic signature, which can bring about various types of healing. Crystal therapy is one of a number of energetic energy healing techniques that can change the frequency at which we vibrate.

ENERGY HEALING THROUGH THE AGES

Our current understanding of energy as a constant force in the universe that is ever changing wasn't articulated until the late nineteenth century. Although people lacked a way to express how energy affects the body in a molecular sense, energy healing modalities were popular across many cultures and eras.

In ancient India (as well as today), practitioners of Ayurveda described the life force that everyone possesses, called prana. Weaknesses and illness result from a lack of prana flowing throughout the body, and so restoring the flow of prana is essential for health. In ancient Chinese medicine, practitioners worked with Chi (or Qi), a life-force energy similar to prana. When the two opposite forces of Chi—yin and yang—were out of balance, illness could result, so therapy sought to rebalance these important forces. (Traditional Chinese Medicine practitioners continue to practice using these principles today.) Ancient Egyptian healers used stones and other energy techniques to diagnose and treat illness, and in ancient Greece, healers believed the body had five humors (types of fluid or temperaments) and that healing involved balancing these humors through medicine and energy work.

In modern times, Mikao Usui, who developed the energy healing technique of Reiki, believed that holy people such as Buddha and Jesus tapped into a universal energy for their healing work.

Chiropractic care is also a modern form of energy work, although those in the profession state they are clearing bony blockages (subluxations) so that nerve energy can flow freely throughout the body. However, the fact that the nerves conduct energy signals shows just how significant a part of our anatomy energy is. Other modern forms of energy healing include Chios, Quantum-Touch, Deeksha, aura cleansing, acupuncture, and many other types of energy medicine that bring about balance and healing emotionally, spiritually, and physically.

What Are Crystals?

Gemologists and geologists define crystals as solid objects with atoms organized in a repeating pattern known as a crystal lattice. There are seven distinct lattice patterns that can be found in crystals. If it doesn't have one of these lattices, a stone is not a crystal. For the purposes of this work, healing crystals may also be defined as minerals, rocks, and gemstones with energetic properties that can influence the human energy field.

MINERALS are naturally occurring substances with a highly ordered pattern that is formed geologically and is typically crystalline in structure. While some minerals have a crystal lattice that classifies them as crystals, not all minerals do.

ROCKS are aggregates of minerals that do not have a single specific physical composition.

GEMSTONES are cut and polished rocks, crystals, or minerals that are attractive and desirable to humans and are therefore assigned a monetary value. Based on quality and rarity, gemstones are classified as either semiprecious or precious. For example, diamonds and rubies are precious gemstones, while garnets and quartz are semiprecious gemstones.

Holy Texts & the Energy Connection

Holy books from various religions discuss the importance of life force (in other words, energy) in the spiritual, emotional, and physical health of humankind.

In the Bible, it says, "That energy is God's energy, an energy deep within you, God himself willing and working at what will give him the most pleasure" (Philippians 2:13). In the Gospel of John, Jesus heals the sick using the energy of God and prayer.

The Hindu Vedas speak of prana—the life force that runs through all living things. According to the Yajur Veda, "There are eleven in the vital energy (prana), existing by their own virtue (ear, skin, eye, tongue, nose, speech, hands, legs, two organs of excretion, and mind: these are organs of perception and volition)."

Buddha also noted energy in defining Seven Factors of Enlightenment: mindfulness, investigation of the dharma [cosmic laws], energy, joy or rapture, relaxation and tranquility, concentration, and equanimity.

The Koran describes God's energy healing the minds, hearts, and bodies of believers: "And when I am ill, it is God who cures me" (The Poets 26:80).

Those who follow Kabbalah, the mystical branch of Judaism, study the Zohar, a collection of commentaries that reveal the spiritual essence of the Torah. The Zohar notes that when the Torah portion known as Pinchas is read aloud once each year during the Sabbath, those who listen with an open heart and remorse for prior misdeeds (even without any knowledge of Hebrew) may experience a great, healing light.

NATURAL VERSUS MAN-MADE

With today's technology, some naturally occurring crystals can be simulated through manufacturing processes. Natural crystals have been formed in the Earth over millions of years, while simulated crystals are created in a laboratory. Natural crystals often have tiny imperfections or inclusions, but their man-made counterparts tend to be flawless. Natural crystals can also be dyed or altered by heat. Altered and manufactured crystals have less monetary value than natural crystals.

While both may be equally beautiful, naturally occurring crystals have stronger healing properties. Man-made crystals may contain much less energy or provide less predictable results. They are not, however, completely without healing energy, but they may react differently or supply weaker energy.

The Power of Crystals

Crystals may help you emotionally, mentally, spiritually, and physically. While the focus in this book is on emotional, mental, and spiritual healing, many people use crystals as complementary therapy to traditional Western medicine when they are experiencing a physical problem or illness. For example, I lie down and place selenite (gypsum) crystals on my forehead for 20 minutes whenever I get a migraine headache. This typically lessens the intensity or makes the headache go away altogether. I always try the selenite before I take any migraine medication or try other therapies. Many other people use crystals in a similar way to help bring about physical healing or an alteration of physical symptoms.

When it comes to emotional, mental, and spiritual healing, the many benefits of crystals include:

CRYSTALS HELP YOU TUNE IN TO YOUR INTUITION. Humans are naturally intuitive, although many of us get so wrapped up in the busyness of our daily lives that we fail to listen to the flashes of insight we receive. You can use crystals to help you focus on the guidance of your inner voice.

CRYSTALS CAN ADD FOCUS TO YOUR MEDITATION, VISUALIZATION, AND AFFIRMATION PRACTICES. If you're struggling to get your life moving in the right direction, meditation, affirmation, and visualization in conjunction with the use of crystals can help focus the energy you need to bring about a desired change. This is a powerful way to direct your energy in a positive direction.

CRYSTALS CAN CLEAR EMOTIONAL BLOCKAGES. Sometimes when we experience emotional trauma, we can create self-protective emotional blockages that prevent us from moving forward in our lives. Working with the right crystals can help clear away these emotional blocks, allowing us to move forward.

CRYSTALS CAN CLEANSE PEOPLE AND SPACES. Many people use crystals for cleansing and clearing away negative energy from spaces or negative thought patterns from people. When I've had a negative experience in my home, I use crystals to cleanse the area and provide protection against future negativity.

CRYSTALS CAN STIMULATE CREATIVITY AND IDEAS. I work with several crystals nearby in my workspace because my job requires a lot of creative thought and movement. By strategically placing crystals in your workspace, you can create an energetic environment that enables you to think and problem solve in a creative manner.

How Crystals Bring About Change

All matter on Earth has a vibrational frequency. Even though we're all made of the same stuff—pure energy—we manage to maintain the illusion of separateness because we vibrate at different frequencies. Vibration is important to who we are, the energy we emit, and the way we relate to one another. We even use a slang term for someone with

The Role of Meditation

Meditation is an important part of performing energy work. I meditate daily and recommend to others daily meditation for 10 to 20 minutes. Meditation helps set intention (the direction you intend your life and actions to take), and it is important in establishing a connection with the energy field, as well as creating receptivity to the energy of crystals or any other form of energy work.

I used to think I couldn't meditate, because I'd sit down to clear my mind and find myself thinking about a dozen different things instead of emptying my mind of all thoughts and "embracing the void." This is very common, and it is one of the main reasons people choose not to meditate—it just seems too difficult.

Clearing your mind isn't always easy. Fortunately, this is not the only way to meditate. There are many types of meditation that you can use to help connect to spiritual energy, including guided imagery, mindfulness meditation, mantra chanting, repetitive or meditative movement, visualization of positive outcomes, or stating affirmations. Each of these forms of meditation can help connect you to your energy field and open you up to the positive effects of the crystals you are using.

MEDITATION FOR CALMNESS

Sit quietly in a comfortable position, in a place where you are unlikely to be disturbed.

Hold an amethyst crystal in your gently clasped hands, which you place in your lap.

Close your eyes and take 10 deep, full breaths, expanding the air fully into your chest.

As you breathe, gently relax your muscle groups, starting at your head and working your way down your body to your feet.

As you inhale, say to yourself, "I inhale peace." As you exhale, say to yourself, "I exhale tension and stress."

Continue for 15 minutes.

MEDITATION FOR FORGIVENESS

Sit quietly in a comfortable position, in a place where you are unlikely to be disturbed.

Hold a rose quartz crystal gently in your hands, and place both hands over the center of your chest at your heart chakra (see page 23).

Close your eyes and breathe gently, noticing your breathing without trying to control it.

Focus your attention on your heart as you repeat the following affirmation to yourself: "I open my heart to love and forgiveness."

Visualize the person you are trying to forgive. In your mind's eye, surround that person in a white light, saying, "I surround you in a white light of love and release you into a positive future."

When you feel ready, open your eyes.

whom we feel an instant affinity, saying we "vibe" with that person. This is a much truer statement than many people realize. As creatures of energy, we tend to attract people, situations, and objects that vibrate at a frequency similar to our own.

However, our vibration varies from day to day and situation to situation, depending on a number of factors such as our mood or emotions, what we put into our bodies, how we care for ourselves, how much time we spend in spiritual pursuits, and the careers and activities we choose. As humans, we are often lightning quick with mood changes and inconsistent in our habits, so our vibrations rise and fall. Lower vibrations tend to lead to less comfortable or painful situations, while higher vibrations help us attract the positive changes we want in our lives.

Unlike humans, crystals maintain a consistent vibration. Because of their crystalline structure, most vibrate at relatively high levels, with certain crystals having extremely high vibrations. When we bring these crystals in contact or proximity to ourselves, we can use them to tune our own vibrations to a higher level. By doing so, we can elevate our mood, focus our mind, and bring about desired change.

Using crystals doesn't have to be difficult. You can hold them in your hands, place them in your pockets, or set them on a desk next to you. You can sleep with them under your pillow or tape some to the bottom of a favorite chair. You can lie supine with crystals placed strategically on your chakras or gently place one over your third eye (see page 23). There aren't many wrong ways to use crystals.

Crystals & Chakras

While you don't need to know or understand chakras to use crystals for healing, combining crystals with chakra work can help make the healing more powerful. With some basic information about chakras, you can leverage the synergy of crystal energy and your chakras to make powerful changes.

WHAT ARE CHAKRAS?

Chakras are energy centers that exist in the body of every human. You have seven chakras that roughly correspond with areas of your body. Each chakra is associated with a color, as well as certain qualities or abilities. The seven chakras are:

FIRST CHAKRA The root or base chakra, which sits at the base of the tailbone

SECOND CHAKRA The sacral chakra, which sits near the belly button

THIRD CHAKRA The solar plexus chakra, which sits at the solar plexus or base of the sternum

FOURTH CHAKRA The heart chakra, which sits in the center of the chest

FIFTH CHAKRA The throat chakra, which sits above the Adam's apple

SIXTH CHAKRA The third eye or brow chakra, which sits in the center of the forehead

SEVENTH CHAKRA The crown chakra, which sits at the top of the head

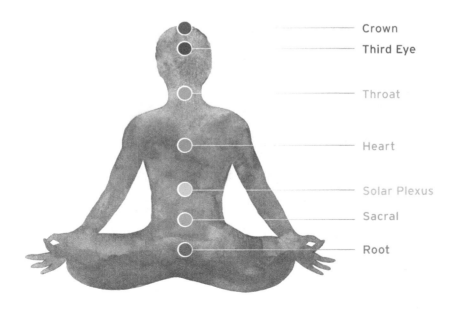

Crown

Third Eye

Throat

Heart

Solar Plexus

Sacral

Root

You have additional chakras as well, that extend out into your energy field, but these are the seven basic chakras that correspond with your physical body. Energy flows through these chakras and throughout your body. Sometimes, one or more of your chakras can become blocked or unbalanced, impeding energy flow. Blockages may occur as a result of trauma, illness, substance use, emotional upset, or other issues.

According to intuitive healer and author Caroline Myss, blockages or imbalances in the chakras may correspond to different physical and emotional problems. For example, blockages of the root chakra, which is related to the sense of belonging in a group, may cause physical and emotional problems such as lower back pain or addiction. Blockages to the heart chakra, which is related to love, may cause heart problems, breast cancer, or the inability to move past grief.

Each of the chakras corresponds to a color or colors. These colors arise from the frequency of the energy vibration of that color. Therefore, when working with crystals and chakras together, choose like colors to help the chakra vibrate at the appropriate frequency.

DIRECTING CRYSTAL HEALING WITH CHAKRAS

When your chakras are blocked, using a crystal that vibrates at the appropriate frequency can help clear the blockage, restoring normal energy flow throughout your body. This can help heal a number of spiritual, emotional, mental, or physical problems that may arise as a result of the blockage.

To use the crystals, lie on your back with your eyes closed and the crystal placed on or touching the corresponding chakra. Visualize the color of the chakra, with energy flowing freely through the chakra.

FIRST CHAKRA (ROOT OR BASE)

COLOR Red
QUALITIES Grounding, connection to emotions, security and safety, finding your place in groups such as families, communities, society
CRYSTALS Garnet, hematite, red calcite, red jasper, obsidian

SECOND CHAKRA (SACRAL)

COLOR Orange
QUALITIES Personal power, sexuality, creativity
CRYSTALS Amber, carnelian, orange calcite, peach moonstone, sunstone

THIRD CHAKRA (SOLAR PLEXUS)

COLOR Yellow
QUALITIES Self-esteem, prosperity, self-identity, moral code
CRYSTALS Amber, citrine, topaz, yellow tigers eye, yellow zircon

FOURTH CHAKRA (HEART)

COLOR Green
QUALITIES Love, balance, forgiveness, integration, compassion
CRYSTALS Emerald, green calcite, green kyanite, peridot, rose quartz

FIFTH CHAKRA (THROAT)

COLOR Blue
QUALITIES Inner truth, self-expression, communication, honesty, integrity
CRYSTALS Blue kyanite, celestite, iolite, lapis, sodalite

SIXTH CHAKRA (THIRD EYE OR BROW)

COLOR Violet/Indigo
QUALITIES Intuition, insight, beliefs and attitudes, mental clarity
CRYSTALS Amethyst, fluorite, lepidolite, sugilite, tanzanite

SEVENTH CHAKRA (CROWN)

COLOR White/Pink/Violet
QUALITIES Connection to spirit/Divine, consciousness, universal connection, oneness
CRYSTALS Clear quartz, Herkimer diamond, labradorite, moonstone, selenite

Crystal Grids

Another way to amplify the power of crystals for healing is by using crystal grids. While using a single crystal is an effective way to modulate energy, using multiple crystals in a grid increases the power exponentially.

WHAT ARE CRYSTAL GRIDS?

Crystal grids are a group of crystals placed in a geometric pattern in a chosen area, such as a tabletop, and programmed with intention to spark healing. To create a crystal grid, you need a minimum of four crystals, although some grids have more. You can use a single type of crystal or a combination of crystals, depending on your intention for the grid. The crystals can be any size or shape (see page 35 for a discussion of shapes). Many people prefer using crystal points to make their grids, because points can focus energy in the direction of the termination, that is, the place where the crystal comes to a point.

Crystal grids can be created to amplify the power of the crystals, to protect or cleanse spaces, or to direct healing toward someone else. The center stone is typically larger than the rest, with smaller stones in a geometric pattern around the center stone. You can create squares, rectangles, circles, rhomboids, triangles, and similar shapes, depending on the number of stones you are using. Although grids don't necessarily have to be geometric, this is a good place to start.

GUIDELINES FOR MAKING A GRID

If you wish to make your own crystal grid, consider the following guidelines.

1. Cleanse and charge the crystals before you start. See page 44 for a discussion of cleansing and charging.

2. Start with a center stone. In general, the center stone may be larger, a different type, or a different shape than the other crystals in the grid.

3. Choose your basic geometric pattern. Place the crystals at even intervals around the center stone to create that pattern. For example, for a square grid, use five stones; place the center stone in the middle and then place four corner stones at equal distances around the center stone to create a square. Always use an equal number of crystals on each side of the pattern to maintain symmetry.

4. After placing the grid, use your finger to trace an imaginary line from one corner stone to the next. Then, trace lines from the center stone to each of the corner stones, creating imaginary spokes.

5. It's okay to leave the grid in place, but you need to cleanse and charge the crystals weekly to maintain its power. Repeat steps one through four when putting the grid back together.

Two Simple Crystal Grids

Try these two grids to see how easy and powerful grids can be to bring about your desired outcome.

PROSPERITY & ABUNDANCE GRID

This small, circular grid draws prosperity into the center stone, and then amplifies it by sending the prosperity out to the immediate area.

TO MAKE THE GRID you'll need a large citrine of any shape and six small clear quartz points.

1. After cleansing the stones, place the citrine in the center and then place each of the quartz points around the citrine in a spoke pattern with the point of each crystal pointing away from the citrine.

2. Trace the lines between the stones as described in step four on page 27.

3. Leave the grid in place for as long as desired to increase prosperity, cleansing the crystals and setting them out again at least once a week.

Citrine is a strong prosperity stone, while clear quartz is an amplifier. Also, specifically using six clear quartz points heightens the intention of abundance, which is one of the qualities associated with the number six in numerology.

LOVE GRID

This grid can help strengthen love relationships or help others find love in their hearts. It uses rose quartz, which is a very powerful (and pretty) love stone.

TO MAKE THE GRID you will need one large round rose quartz crystal and 12 small rose quartz beads or crystals of any shape.

1. After cleansing the crystals, place the large round rose quartz crystal on your surface.

2. Arrange the smaller stones around it in an infinity symbol (a sideways figure eight) with six crystals on either side and the large crystal as the center point of the symbol.

3. Trace the lines between the stones as described in step four on page 27.

4. Leave the grid in place for as long as desired, cleansing the crystals and setting them out again at least once a week.

The rose quartz triggers love, while the infinity symbol represents lasting love.

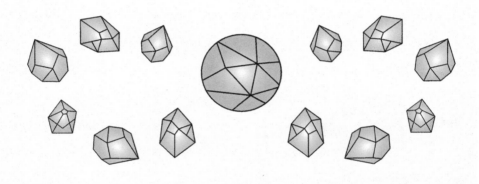

2
CHAPTER

Shopping for Crystals

*S*hopping for crystals is a fun activity. Part of the enjoyment comes from personally choosing crystals for your collection. There are many types of stores that sell crystals, such as dedicated crystal stores, New Age shops, bead stores, hobby shops, Wiccan stores, and metaphysical shops. You may also be able to find crystals at traveling rock, gem, and mineral shows; swap meets; fairs; and similar events.

Inside the Crystal Shop

Just like any new experience, shopping for crystals may seem a bit daunting at first. Shops that sell crystals often offer a number of other items for sale related to New Age or metaphysical practices, such as incense, candles, statues, reference books, and oracle cards. As you walk through the door, your eye will likely be drawn to many different types of crystals and products.

How a shop organizes its crystal displays varies from place to place. Some of the more expensive specimens, such as crystals cut into spheres and pyramids, large point clusters, or gemstone jewelry may be locked in glass display cases. Smaller crystals are typically displayed in open containers so you can sift through them to find the perfect fit without asking for assistance.

Buying Crystals for Someone Else

Occasionally, you may wish to buy a crystal for someone else. This can be tricky, since crystal energy resonates differently with different people, but you can still give a crystal as a gift. In fact, I buy crystals for friends all the time. If I am giving a crystal for healing purposes, I base my selection on the issues the friend is currently dealing with and choose a crystal that will best fit the situation. I still perform a touch test. However, instead of thinking of myself, I set the intention of selecting a crystal for my friend, and then I visualize that friend as I hold each crystal and mentally ask if the crystal is right for that person. Feeling positive emotions, just as you'd hope to feel when considering a crystal for yourself, is a good indicator.

While in the shop, you can browse or ask questions. If you are interested in purchasing a crystal you see in a locked case, don't hesitate to ask to hold it. Finding a vibrational affinity for the crystal you choose is an important part of the process. Many of the salespeople at these shops are well versed in the use of crystals and can help you find the perfect crystals for your needs.

Common Shapes

Crystals come in many colors, cuts, sizes, and shapes. Some are completely natural and look just like rocks, while others are cut and polished into an array of shapes. When you are shopping for crystals, you'll likely find a wide variety of the following types.

ROUGH STONES are uncut and unpolished, and sold in their naturally occurring forms. They may be more opaque than their cut and polished counterparts. Although some may look like the rocks you'd find anywhere in nature, they still have the properties of cut and polished crystals.

TUMBLED STONES are small rough stones that have been placed in a rock tumbler to round out the edges, producing a smooth, shiny finish. This brings out the color and natural pattern of the crystals. These may also be called polished stones, though polishing can also be done by hand or another method.

POINTS occur naturally on one end of some crystals, due to the crystalline structure (some are cut to a point). The points may be polished or unpolished. Using a crystal point is a good way to direct energy either away from the body or toward the body by pointing it in the desired direction.

CLUSTERS are naturally occurring formations that consist of several crystal points projecting from a rock base. Clusters work well for directing energy into the space in which they sit.

GEODES are rocks that contain a small cavity that is lined with crystals. Geodes are usually sliced in half to reveal the crystals inside a generally rough outer shell.

SLABS are cross-cut disks of certain types of crystals, such as agates. Sometimes geodes are also sliced into disks.

WANDS are smooth, oblong, polished crystals with rounded ends. They may be wider at one end than the other, or they may taper to a dull point at one end. Many people use wands for massage, because they are helpful for channeling energy.

PYRAMIDS, CUBES, SPHERES, HEARTS, AND STARS are among the many shapes crystals can be cut and polished into. Choose a shape that you feel drawn to.

How to Choose a Crystal

Choosing a crystal is unique to each individual, because crystals may vibrate differently with different people's energy. Be sure to pay close attention to your inner voice when choosing a crystal. Making a selection that feels good to you is an intuitive process.

COLOR ATTRACTION

One of the first keys to choosing a crystal for yourself is attraction. Walk through the aisles of the crystal shop, visually scanning all of the offerings. Note colors that jump out at you. If you are drawn to a particular color of crystal, then you can look at other crystals within that shade. For instance, if red crystals attract you, take a closer look at gemstones such as garnet, red jasper, bloodstone, and sardonyx. As you examine crystals in that color range, note specific crystals that draw you to them, making you want to take a closer look or touch them.

PHYSICAL SENSATION

After making your visual selection, do a touch test. This is one of the most important tests for choosing a crystal. Much to my family's consternation, I've been known to spend a long time picking up and holding different stones to find those that resonate with me.

Hold the crystal in the palm of your receiving hand (your nondominant hand, so if you are right handed, this is your left hand, and vice versa), close your eyes, and notice how the crystal feels there. If it creates an unpleasant sensation, put it back and choose another. If it creates a pleasant or neutral sensation, continue your test.

After noting how your hand feels, expand your focus to the rest of your body. Do you notice any physical sensations? How do you feel emotionally when you hold the crystal? How do you feel mentally? Use all these questions to evaluate whether the crystal is right for you. A good match is a crystal that makes you feel balanced, grounded, clear, peaceful, happy, or other positive emotions or sensations.

Finally, it's okay to ask yourself silently, "Is this the crystal for me?" I do this with every crystal I am considering. I ask myself the question, and then I stand with my eyes closed and wait for the answer. Typically, the answer I'm seeking is the first thought that pops into my mind. Listen to your inner voice in this manner as you interact with the crystal to make your decision.

COST

When evaluating any purchase, cost usually plays a role. Crystals range in price from a few dollars to three figures (or more for extremely large or rare specimens). If you find a crystal that feels really good but it's not in your budget, you can look for smaller versions of that crystal, which may be less expensive. Generally, if you're on a budget, it's best to choose among crystals that cost under $20. Tumbled stones are a good, relatively inexpensive option if you plan to buy several different stones. Feel free to pay more if a specific crystal is rare or large and truly feels like it belongs with you.

SIZE

Larger pieces of crystals tend to generate more energy and, as a result, a more profound power. However, even the smallest crystal can be extremely effective, so small crystals will work well for most people's needs. If you are considering the same crystal in two different sizes, don't let size alone determine which you purchase. If you connect more immediately with the sensation of the smaller stone, that is likely the one that will work more effectively for you.

Crystal Jewelry

Natural gemstones in jewelry still carry the same healing potential as crystals sold individually. When you purchase a piece of jewelry with one or more gemstones in it, you have beautiful, wearable art that also imparts healing properties; whether the jewelry was marketed as a healing crystal or not, it has the same vibrational energy. This only works with natural gemstones, however, and not with synthetic or altered stones.

When you purchase a piece of gemstone jewelry, cleanse it in a manner similar to a regular crystal cleansing (see page 44), taking precautions to protect the nongemstone elements of the piece. Then feel free to wear it for healing purposes. By cleansing the gemstones once a week, you can maintain the healing properties of the jewelry.

Choosing Multiple Crystals

If you are just getting started with crystal healing, you may wish to buy multiple crystals to work with a variety of issues. Multiple crystals enable you to capitalize on the synergy between the energy of crystals (see chapter 4 for remedies involving more than one crystal used to address a particular problem or goal) or balance your chakras. Multiple crystals make it possible for you to put together crystal grids or simply enable you to get started with a few different (and beautiful) options.

CRYSTAL STARTER KITS

Crystal healing starter kits are available from various vendors. These kits may contain anywhere from a few common stones to as many as 30. Smaller starter kits may cost $15 to $20, while larger starter kits may cost $100 or more. Some starter kits are specific to the chakras and may contain one to three crystals for use with each chakra.

If you purchase a starter kit, you don't have to spend your time selecting individual crystals. However, because you don't have the luxury of feeling how each crystal interacts with your energy field, this can be a disadvantage. I'm not a huge fan of starter kits for this reason, but if you're looking for a quick way to get your collection started, a starter kit may be the way you choose to go.

MAKE YOUR OWN STARTER KIT

You can make your own starter kit containing the essential crystals that everyone should have in their collection for crystal healing work. You can keep the kit affordable by selecting smaller stones. Five crystals to have on hand include:

- Clear quartz
- Amethyst
- Citrine
- Rose quartz
- Smoky quartz

To put together a *chakra* starter kit, consider these stones (or any of the other crystals listed for each chakra on page 24):

- First chakra (root or base): Red jasper
- Second chakra (sacral): Carnelian
- Third chakra (solar plexus): Citrine
- Fourth chakra (heart): Green aventurine
- Fifth chakra (throat): Sodalite
- Sixth chakra (third eye or brow): Amethyst
- Seventh chakra (crown): Clear quartz

Buyer Beware

When you're shopping, you'll want to avoid some common pitfalls associated with buying crystals. Keep the following in mind before you make your purchase.

SOME CRYSTALS ARE SYNTHETIC OR MAN-MADE. If a crystal seems to be too perfect or flawless, it may be manufactured. Talk with the salesperson and ask about the source of the crystal. You can still purchase the piece if you'd like, but it is important to know what you are buying and how useful it will be for your purposes.

NOT ALL CITRINE IS NATURAL. Much of what may look like citrine is actually amethyst that has been heated until it turns yellow. This changes the properties of the crystal somewhat, so be sure to ask if a specific crystal is natural citrine, if that is the stone you want.

BEWARE OF TRADEMARK-NAMED STONES WITH A HIGHER PRICE TAG.
Stones with a name that has been trademarked are just other stones that have been given marketing-friendly names, which may make them more expensive but not more powerful. This doesn't mean trademarked stones are bad or ineffective, just that they may be more expensive than their non-trademarked counterparts. Trademarked stones include Infinite Stones, Boji Stones, Azeztulite, and many others.

SOME CRYSTALS HAVE BEEN ALTERED FROM THEIR NATURAL STATE.
Be sure to ask the salesperson if the crystal has had any treatments, such as dyeing, heat treating, or coating. These may alter the properties of the crystals. For example, howlite can be dyed to look like turquoise, but these stones have different properties. If you are in the market for turquoise (or any stone, for that matter), it is important to ask if it is a naturally occurring crystal in its unaltered form.

3

CHAPTER

Preparing to Use Crystals

After carefully selecting my crystals and bringing them home, I immediately start preparing to use them by cleansing, charging, and programming them. Your crystal energy work will benefit if you do the same. A big part of using crystals rests with how you set your intentions. Properly preparing your crystals, the space where you use them, and your mind can help you set your intention, allowing you to make the most of their energetic healing properties.

Cleansing Your Crystals

Due to their energetic nature, crystals hold on to energy patterns with which they come in contact. By the time your crystals have made their way to you, they have been in many hands and places. This is why it is important to cleanse your crystals. I recommend cleansing them as soon as you bring them home, and then cleansing them at least weekly, or more frequently for those you use daily. There are several methods for cleansing crystals.

SALT WATER Nonporous crystals, such as quartz and amethyst, can be soaked in a saltwater solution. Submerge your crystals in the salt water for about an hour (longer if the crystals have had heavy use), and then rinse them and pat them dry. Use sea salt or Himalayan pink salt for this task, not table salt. Do not use this method for porous crystals, such as selenite, desert rose, and gypsum. You'll also want to keep magnetic stones, such as lodestone, out of salt water because it could rust the stone.

Is It Possible to Ruin a Crystal?

Crystals are hardy. They never lose their energy, regardless of their shape or condition. Even if they break, they still work well after cleansing and charging. For example, a piece of black tourmaline I was carrying in my pocket broke in half when I came into contact with an extremely negative person. After I discovered the broken tourmaline, I cleansed and charged both pieces, and each piece was good as new.

Really, the only way to harm a crystal in terms of how it works for you is by failing to cleanse and charge it. However, once you do, it will be back in full working order.

SMOKE Light a bundle of sage, cedar, lavender, or sweetgrass, and blow out the flame. Then hold the crystals in the stream of smoke to cleanse them. (I use a combination of these four herbs.) You can also cleanse them in the smoke from incense, such as Nag Champa sticks.

QUARTZ CLUSTERS OR GEODES If you have a large cluster or geode made of a quartz stone, such as amethyst or clear quartz, you can place your smaller crystals in the cavity for 24 hours to cleanse them.

ENERGY If you have some type of energy healing ability (such as Reiki), you can cleanse the crystals using that energy. As a Reiki master, I do this by holding the crystals in my giving (dominant) hand and sending Reiki energy to them.

Charging & Programming Your Crystals

After cleansing, you need to charge your crystals. Charging puts energy back into the crystals so they can continue to function at their highest level. You should charge your crystals every time you cleanse them. Programming your crystals involves placing intention into them for the specific task you'd like them to complete. This can help the crystal work more effectively, so do this every time you cleanse and charge them. You can use several methods for these purposes. Consider the following ideas.

To charge your crystals in nature, you can place them outside in the sunlight or moonlight for 6 to 12 hours. You can also charge your crystals with visualization. Hold the crystal or crystals in your giving (dominant) hand. Close your eyes and visualize white light coming down from the universe, entering through your crown chakra, traveling down through each of your chakras, then into your arm and hand, and then from your hand into the crystal. Do this for about 10 minutes.

To program the crystal once it has been charged, repeat the visualization process described, but this time, focus on the type of energy you'd like the crystal to have.

Preparing Your Space

Creating an environment for your crystal work can help you set your intention for success. I have a small space dedicated to my energy healing work that is free of distractions and energetic disturbances. It is an electronics-free zone, as well as a quiet and comfortable place where I won't be disturbed.

When setting up your workspace, make it comfortable. Consider the following tips:

- Create a space where you can sit and/or lie comfortably for meditation.

- Use soft lighting, possibly on a dimmer.

- Remove distractions.

- Minimize objects that may disrupt or disturb energy flow, such as computers, tablets, or cell phones.

- Keep the tools you will need nearby, such as candles, incense, and sage.

- Decorate your space with beloved objects that make you feel happy, peaceful, and positive.

- Once your space is set up, clear the energy by using the space cleansing remedies on page 72. Whenever the area starts to feel congested, cleanse the space again.

- Keep negativity out of your space. For example, don't pay bills or fight with your spouse in that area.

- Dedicate your space—no matter how small—to energetically positive activities such as meditation, visualization, and crystal healing.

Preparing Your Mind

Preparing your mind for crystal healing and other energy work is essential for setting your intentions for the work you are about to do. It creates a positive and affirmative space for the crystals' energy to work with you. You may want to meditate (see page 21), pray, or chant a mantra—whatever puts you in a positive and spiritual mind-set and clears away any lingering negativity. You may also wish to begin with an affirmation, such as, "I am grateful that the work I do today with these crystals brings me positive, healing vibrations."

Five More Crystals That Should Be in Every Home

Along with the healing crystals starter kit on page 39, there are several other crystals that have properties that will work well in most homes. Consider adding the following five crystals to your collection.

AMETRINE is a wonderful mix of citrine and amethyst, so it has the healing and energetic qualities of both crystals.

GREEN AVENTURINE is a prosperity and abundance crystal, which can help you prosper in finances, health, happiness, and well-being.

YELLOW TIGERS EYE is a stone of luck and protection.

RAINBOW FLUORITE contains multiple colors, so it vibrates in tune with multiple energies, including health, intuition, serenity, creativity, and spirituality.

BLUE CHALCEDONY enhances relationships by strengthening compassion and unconditional love.

4
CHAPTER

Crystal Remedies for Mind, Heart & Soul

When you are dealing with spiritual, mental, or emotional issues, or when you aspire to bring positive change in your life, you may find the remedies in this chapter quite helpful. The remedies are not meant to replace the advice or treatment of a qualified health care professional, of course, but they can be a powerful helper to the more traditional steps you may be taking to resolve a particular challenge. As you already know, change tends not to happen overnight. Remedies can and should be repeated as needed, as part of an ongoing healing process.

Abandonment

Feelings of abandonment may arise from the recent loss of a relationship, or they may stem from childhood loss. However a sense of abandonment comes about, it can leave you feeling lost, alone, and empty. Using the mantra to remind yourself that your true source of unconditional love lies within, while working with the crystal remedies, can be a source of emotional and spiritual support during these difficult times.

I give myself unconditional love and receive unconditional love from the universe.

MEDITATION

Meditate using the mantra while holding rose quartz, which is a stone of unconditional love. Picture yourself wrapped in a warm, pink light as you meditate. Continue for at least 10 minutes or until you feel a sense of peace.

REMEDY #1: MULTI-STONE SUPPORTIVE GRID

Set up a crystal grid near where you work or sleep. Place the rose quartz as a center stone, and surround it with a square of Apache tears, amazonite, garnet, and carnelian. For this grid, you can use either rough, uncut stones or unshaped, polished stones, depending on what you have available.

- **ROSE QUARTZ** for unconditional love
- **APACHE TEARS** for releasing feelings of grief
- **AMAZONITE** for healing emotional pain
- **GARNET** for healing issues of belonging
- **CARNELIAN** for self-empowerment

REMEDY #2: ROSE QUARTZ, CITRINE & OBSIDIAN CHAKRA WORK

Lie on your back in a comfortable position. Place a rose quartz stone on your heart chakra, citrine on your solar plexus chakra, and obsidian on your root chakra. Breathe deeply and repeat the mantra 10 times, or until you notice a sense of peace.

TIP: If you're unsure why you are feeling abandoned, close your eyes and ask yourself from where your sense of abandonment arises. Sit quietly and see what you notice. Sometimes the best way to release a feeling is to recognize its source and acknowledge it.

Abundance

While many people associate abundance with financial wealth, in this context it means an abundance of all the good life has to offer. Abundance can include wealth, health, joy, love, compassion, family, creativity, and all of the other positive attributes you wish to experience in your life.

I am grateful to the universe, which provides me with an abundance of all I need.

MEDITATION

Sit in a comfortable position holding a clear quartz crystal, which will amplify your visualizations. Visualize yourself living a life of abundance in all ways, making the vision as clear and real as possible. When you have completed your visualization, repeat the mantra to yourself nine times (in numerology, nine is an abundance number).

REMEDY #1: CITRINE

Place a piece of citrine in the prosperity corner of your home. To find the prosperity corner, stand with your back to the front door, facing into your home. The farthest back left corner is your prosperity corner. I have a citrine cluster in the back of my bedroom closet for this very reason.

REMEDY #2: GARNET ROOT CHAKRA WORK

Blocked abundance and lack consciousness (believing there is not enough) is a root chakra issue. Lie on your back with a garnet on your root chakra. Close your eyes and breathe deeply, repeating the mantra for at least 10 minutes.

 TIP: Abundance responds to the Law of Attraction (the belief that we attract what we focus our energy on), so how you speak, think, and believe can greatly affect the abundance you experience in life. One of the biggest blocks to receiving abundance is the belief that there is a finite amount of whatever you wish to receive in the universe. When you believe there is only so much to go around, it limits what the universe provides. When you catch yourself thinking about lack or limitations on abundance, immediately stop that thought and repeat the mantra to yourself 10 times, or until you feel a sense of peace.

Abuse

Abuse, whether emotional, mental, or physical, can leave lasting scars. Many people carry the effects of abuse with them, essentially becoming their own tormentor long after any outside abuse has ceased. While the work in this section is effective for all types of abuse, different types may cause energetic blockages in different chakras. For instance, sexual abuse may affect your root chakra, while abuse at the hands of a parent may bring up sacral or solar plexus chakra issues. These remedies are intended for people who are grappling with past abuse. If you are currently suffering from abuse, seeking professional help is an important first step.

I release the pain of my past for a more positive and loving future.

MEDITATION

Close your eyes and allow yourself to feel the grief and pain of your past abuse. Notice where in your body you feel that pain. Inhale deeply and imagine loving light coming in with the breath and flowing to wherever you feel your pain. Then exhale and repeat the mantra. Continue for at least 10 minutes or until you feel a sense of peace.

REMEDY #1: GARNET

Garnet is a powerful root chakra stone that can help you release past pain and reclaim personal power. Carry a garnet with you in your pocket, tape one to the bottom of your work chair, or keep one next to your bed.

REMEDY #2: MULTI-STONE CHAKRA WORK

Abuse affects several chakras, so meditating with stones on the affected chakras can help clear blockages that result from the abuse. Lie on your back with some or all of these stones on the corresponding chakras. Feel free to pick and choose chakras based on where you feel you are experiencing issues related to your abuse.

- Garnet on your root chakra, which is where your sense of belonging and self-identity lie
- Carnelian on your sacral chakra, which is the center of your personal power
- Yellow tigers eye on your solar plexus chakra to support self-esteem and formation of healthy boundaries
- Rose quartz on your heart chakra to support unconditional love
- Lapis lazuli on your throat chakra to support speaking your truth

 TIP: Many people try to avoid the pain from past abuse by ignoring or repressing it. Unfortunately, this can make the pain burrow even deeper and become fixed. While it may seem scary to deal with the pain of abuse, acknowledging that pain and sending unconditional love to yourself are the first steps in overcoming it.

Acceptance/ Surrender

In his book *The Power of Now*, Eckhart Tolle discusses the origins of pain, contending that all emotional and spiritual pain arises because we get stuck reliving the past or worrying about the future, rather than surrendering to the now. This is also a central tenet of Buddhism. When difficult things happen in our lives, acceptance may be difficult, but refusing to accept what has happened leaves us stuck in pain and negativity. Acceptance and surrender are big steps in moving forward.

I accept the moment as it is and release anything I do not have the power to change.

MEDITATION

Close your eyes and sit comfortably. Focus on your current situation, noticing where the feelings of pain are located in your body. Now, while repeating the mantra, imagine that pain as a black mass that begins to dissolve as you breathe in white light. Exhale and picture the black vapors lifting out of your body and dissolving into the universe. Do this for about 10 minutes, or until you feel a sense of peace.

REMEDY #1: APATITE

Apatite is the stone of acceptance. Keep a piece tucked into a pocket near your heart or wear a piece around your neck.

REMEDY #2: APACHE TEARS

These smooth stones are effective for relieving disappointment and turning it to acceptance. Hold Apache tears in your hand as you repeat this verse of the Serenity Prayer.

> *God grant me the serenity*
> *to accept the things I cannot change,*
> *the courage to change the things I can,*
> *and the wisdom to know the difference.*

 TIP: Many people believe that to surrender shows weakness, but it is actually a sign of strength. Allowing yourself to surrender to those things you cannot change empowers you to focus your energy on taking positive steps toward the future.

Addiction

Whether you're addicted to a substance, an activity, an idea, or something else, addiction can quickly throw you and your life completely out of balance. While many physical addictions require therapy or treatment, supporting yourself spiritually and emotionally can help ease that process.

I am free of my desire for [name the addiction]. I release it, and it releases me.

MEDITATION

Addiction can bring about an imbalance in all the chakras, so meditating on the mantra while lying with chakra stones on each chakra may be helpful to restore balance. You can also work specific chakras when dealing with addiction. For example, place a carnelian on your sacral chakra and lapis lazuli on your throat chakra. These are the two chakras that deal with willpower and addiction. Perform the meditation for at least 10 minutes.

REMEDY #1: LABRADORITE

Carry or wear labradorite as you go throughout your days of addiction work. It can help detoxify you energetically from the effects of alcohol or drugs, and it can help reduce self-destructive behaviors. You may also sleep with labradorite under your pillow. If you go to rehab, keep labradorite with you to support you in the detoxification process. Cleanse the labradorite daily to rid it of the heavy energy associated with addiction issues.

REMEDY #2: AMETHYST

Amethyst is known as the sober stone, and it has long been believed that amethyst can assist with sobriety. Wear amethyst jewelry or carry amethyst in your pocket for support during withdrawal and to temper addictive tendencies and behaviors. You can also create an amethyst grid in any geometric shape that feels powerful to you, for more control and energy.

 TIP: Addiction often has underlying issues, such as grief, anger, resentment, past abuse, or others. Along with working through the addiction remedies, consider using the remedies for the underlying issues, as well. For example, if your addiction is a way to dull the pain of past abuse, try the remedies listed under Abuse.

Anger

Anger is a natural and acceptable emotion. When we allow ourselves to fully experience anger, it can easily pass through our bodies and dissipate. However, sometimes we get stuck in anger until it hardens into resentment. Know that holding on to anger doesn't hurt the object of your ire. It only harms you, so it is important to release the anger and move on with your life.

I breathe in peace. I release anger.

MEDITATION

Perform this meditation in a sitting position. Place both hands gently over your solar plexus chakra. Take a deep breath. As you inhale, imagine peace flowing into your body and say aloud or to yourself, "I breathe in peace." Exhale and picture your anger flowing out of your body through your nose. As you exhale say, "I release anger." Do this for 10 minutes or until you feel peaceful.

REMEDY #1: CARNELIAN

Carnelian is a calming and grounding stone that can help you release anger quickly. When you are angry, hold the stone in your hand and allow yourself to fully experience the anger until it dissipates.

REMEDY #2: AMBER & BLACK TOURMALINE

If anger or negativity is directed toward you from another, wear amber jewelry or carry a piece of amber in your pocket to absorb the negativity and anger so that you don't absorb it yourself. You can also carry a piece of black tourmaline, which will completely block the negativity from reaching you. During meditation, hold the amber in your receiving (nondominant) hand and the black tourmaline in your giving (dominant) hand, feeling positive energy flowing from the amber and negative energy flowing into the black tourmaline.

 TIP: Don't try to avoid getting angry; it is a necessary emotion. In the moment, allow yourself to fully experience and express your anger so that you can release it and move forward.

Anxiety

While it's natural to feel anxious from time to time, persistent anxiety can keep you from living your best life. Living in a heightened state of anxiety can tax you physically and emotionally, taking a toll on your body, overworking your adrenal glands, and throwing your hormones out of balance. Anxiety may take many forms, such as social anxiety, phobias, constant worry, or obsessions and compulsions. Anxiety is a root chakra issue that relates to a sense of security, so working with this chakra can help you feel more secure.

I relax into infinite serenity.

MEDITATION

Sit quietly while holding a root chakra stone, such as a garnet. Close your eyes and breathe in. As you breathe in, visualize peace flowing into your body and say the mantra. Now, as you exhale fully, visualize your anxiety flowing out of you. Continue for at least 10 minutes or until your anxiety subsides.

REMEDY #1: BLUE LACE AGATE

Blue lace agate has a serene blue color that is reflective of its calming properties. Wearing or carrying blue lace agate in your pocket can help ease situational anxiety, such as nerves for a job interview or travel-related stress.

REMEDY #2: LAPIS LAZULI & CLEAR QUARTZ GRID

Create a circular grid with a large lapis lazuli center stone of any shape and eight clear quartz points arranged in a circle around the lapis. Face the quartz points away from the lapis toward the room. The quartz will amplify the calming properties of the lapis and send them out into the surrounding area.

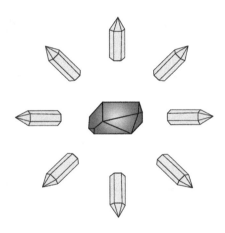

REMEDY #3: BLACK TOURMALINE

Carry black tourmaline in your pocket when you are feeling anxious. It is a grounding stone that will absorb any negativity.

SETTING

Boundaries

Setting appropriate boundaries is important for your own well-being, as well as for establishing healthy relationships. To set boundaries with others, you first need to understand your own limits. By knowing your limits and setting boundaries, you teach others how you wish to be treated. Sometimes, because we want others to like us, it may be difficult to set and hold boundaries, but doing so is an essential step in learning to respect ourselves and our relationships.

I assert myself with kindness, compassion, and confidence.

MEDITATION

Your solar plexus chakra is the source of your self-identification, which is where you will learn and understand your own personal boundaries. You will communicate your boundaries with integrity from your throat chakra. Lie comfortably on your back with your hands lightly resting on your solar plexus chakra. Close your eyes and focus your attention on your solar plexus chakra. With your eyes closed, inhale deeply and ask, "What are my boundaries?" Lie, breathing normally with your focus on your solar plexus chakra, until you feel you know the answer. Now, gently slide your hands up your midline to rest gently over your throat chakra and repeat the mantra 10 times, or until you feel a sense of peace.

REMEDY #1: CITRINE

When you're trying to learn what your boundaries are, place a piece of citrine under your pillow. As you drift off to sleep, ask the universe to help you understand your boundaries. When you wake up, write down what you have discovered. Repeat this nightly for at least a week.

REMEDY #2: SODALITE & ROSE QUARTZ

Once you are firm in what your boundaries are, use rose quartz to impart compassion and sodalite to enhance and clarify communication. Carrying these two crystals with you in a pocket whenever you need to assert your boundaries will help you do so with kindness, clarity, and love.

Centering

Centering is the process of calming your mind, body, and spirit and moving into your peaceful center. When you are centered, you are in a calm and relaxed state, but you are also alert. From this state, it is easier to understand the flow of energy and information around you, and it is easier to tune in to your creativity, feelings, and intuition, as well as to receive information from the Divine.

I relax my mind, body, and spirit and find my center.

MEDITATION

Sit comfortably with your eyes closed. Notice your breathing. As you begin to relax, repeat the mantra several times until you feel relaxed, maintaining focus on your center, the area between your solar plexus and sacral chakras.

REMEDY #1: BLUE LACE AGATE

Blue lace agate is a calming stone that can also help you center yourself. Hold the stone in one hand and, with your eyes closed, breathe deeply, allowing calm to wash over you. You can remain in any position, even standing, to center yourself this way. If you tend to be off center a lot, it may be helpful to carry a piece of blue lace agate with you to hold whenever you need to find your center.

REMEDY #2: CLEAR QUARTZ

Center yourself at the start of the day with a brief clear quartz meditation. Sit comfortably, holding a piece of clear quartz in your receiving (nondominant) hand. Close your eyes and take 10 deep, full breaths, focusing your attention on your core and feeling the energy from the clear quartz flowing toward your center.

 TIP: Typically, grounding and centering are activities you perform together. Always ground yourself (see page 128) before centering.

ACCEPTING

Change

Many people find change difficult because they fear the unknown. They prefer to remain with something they know, even if it brings them pain or discomfort, rather than face an uncertain future. However, change is a necessary and natural part of life. The nature of the universe is constant change, and without it, we can't grow.

I am grateful for change in my life because it serves as a source of positive empowerment.

MEDITATION

Sit quietly in a comfortable position with your eyes closed. Place both hands gently over your heart chakra. Breathe deeply and visualize pure white energy flowing from above, down through your crown chakra, through your arms and hands, and into your heart chakra. Repeat the mantra, sitting quietly for at least 10 minutes or until you feel at peace.

REMEDY #1: WATERMELON TOURMALINE

During periods of tumultuous change in your life, carry a piece of watermelon tourmaline in your pocket or wear watermelon tourmaline in a necklace. It will help bring acceptance and clarity to your situation.

REMEDY #2: PREHNITE & CLEAR QUARTZ GRID

Set up a simple grid with a prehnite center stone and three clear quartz points arranged in a triangle around the center stone, with the points facing away from the center. The quartz points will amplify the power of the prehnite, which provides inner strength and acceptance of new circumstances. The direction of the quartz points moves the energy in the direction the point faces, in this case, sending it out into the surrounding area.

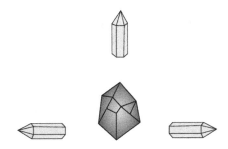

BRINGING ABOUT
Change

Sometimes you reach a place in your life where you are stuck in a rut, and you know you must change. However, it can be difficult to actually take the steps required for change, because you are so comfortable where you are. Everyone needs a little help to get started from time to time, but once you do, you'll discover that the effort you made to change was worthwhile.

I have the motivation to make the changes necessary for my growth.

MEDITATION

Sit comfortably with your eyes closed. Breathe naturally, relaxing your body and mind. Visualize the aspect of yourself you'd like to change, and imagine yourself making the change, taking the visualization through to its logical conclusion. Allow yourself to feel the joy and empowerment that comes from making that change. After your visualization, repeat the mantra nine times (in numerology, nine is the number of completion).

REMEDY #1: BLUE OR GREEN AVENTURINE

Blue and green aventurine are stones of opportunity, and change is always about opportunity. Sleep with a blue or green aventurine under your pillow to help you subconsciously awaken your will to bring about change.

REMEDY #2: BLUE KYANITE

Use blue kyanite to help dissolve old habits and beliefs, which often block you from making changes in your life. Meditate holding a blue kyanite crystal in your receiving (nondominant) hand. As you breathe in, repeat, "I welcome new ideas that serve me," and as you breathe out, repeat, "I release that which is no longer useful to me."

 TIP: Most often, it is your mind-set that prevents change. It may help to think of change in a different way. Instead of considering change as a necessary evil or something to fear, set your mind to believe that change is always an opportunity to bring positive, new energy into your life.

Cleansing

Cleansing a new space can help make it your own, removing any negativity from past inhabitants. Cleansing is an excellent way to prepare a new home or apartment, a new office or classroom, or any other space where you spend a lot of time. You can also use it to refresh a space after a period of negativity, such as a fight with a loved one or an illness.

The light of love fills this space.

MEDITATION

Sit in the center of the space with your eyes closed, breathing normally. Visualize a white light coming down from above and filling the space all around you, pushing out any previous energy. As you visualize, repeat the mantra for 10 minutes or until your intuition tells you the space has been cleansed.

REMEDY #1: CLEAR QUARTZ

Place a clear quartz cluster in a central location, or strategically place pieces of clear quartz around the room (or both). Once the quartz is in place, stand in the center of the room with your eyes closed. Do the meditation with the quartz in place.

REMEDY #2: BLACK TOURMALINE AFTER SMUDGING

Light a smudge bundle of sage and cedar, sage and sweetgrass, or sage and lavender. Blow out the bundle but leave it smoldering. Working clockwise, carry the smoking bundle around the room's perimeter and wave it clockwise around every door and window. Visualize pure light entering the room while repeating the mantra. After you've smudged the entire space, place black tourmaline pieces in the four corners of the area to block negative energy from entering.

SPIRITUAL AND/OR EMOTIONAL

Cleansing

Just as you need to bathe to cleanse your physical body, sometimes you may also feel in need of an emotional or spiritual cleansing. Using cleansing techniques can help remove any lingering negativity, leaving you feeling refreshed and renewed. Consider cleansing after periods of negativity, or if you're just feeling that you need to refresh your intuition, creativity, or some other aspect of yourself. I cleanse after interacting with a negative person, which always helps me wash away their energy and focus on my own.

I fill myself with a pure, cleansing white light.

MEDITATION

Close your eyes and visualize a white light coming down from above and entering into your body through your crown chakra. Now, visualize the white light traveling downward through each chakra and passing all the way through you into the Earth. Perform this meditation for about 10 minutes.

REMEDY #1: CLEAR & SMOKY QUARTZ

Dissolve ¼ cup of Himalayan pink salt or sea salt in a full bathtub. Sit in the tub and add a clear quartz crystal and a smoky quartz crystal to the water. Soak for 10 minutes with your eyes closed, repeating the mantra. Remove the crystals from the tub and then drain it, remaining in the tub until all the water drains away. Afterward, cleanse your crystals (see page 44).

REMEDY #2: SELENITE

Use selenite when you meditate, to increase the cleansing effects of your meditation. During meditation, hold the selenite in your receiving (nondominant) hand or lie on the floor and place it in contact with your crown chakra. You can do this with a piece also touching your root chakra, letting the energy run through your chakras to cleanse them.

REMEDY #3: BLOODSTONE

Bloodstone can help cleanse your aura. Hold a bloodstone in your receiving (nondominant) hand and close your eyes. Visualize pure white energy coming from the stone and spreading into your body and then out into your aura.

Comfort

During difficult times, we often turn to other people or objects for comfort. While relationships with others are an important part of being human, you can be your own greatest source of comfort during times of sorrow. Using crystals can help you realize that your most important source of comfort lies within you, helping you connect to your own Divine source of power to bring about peace and acceptance.

I am grateful to the Divine, my source of comfort.

MEDITATION

Sit comfortably with your eyes closed, placing your receiving (non-dominant) hand on your head and your giving (dominant) hand on your heart. Breathing naturally and, repeating the mantra, visualize a gentle green light coming down from above and entering through your crown chakra. Allow the light to flow down through the chakras into your heart, as well as through your arms and hands into your heart chakra. Sit this way for at least 10 minutes or until you feel comfort.

REMEDY #1: SELENITE & GREEN AVENTURINE CHAKRA WORK

Communication with the Divine comes from your crown chakra and flows down into your heart chakra. Use this crystal meditation to draw peace in through your crown chakra and send emotional soothing into your heart chakra. Lie on your back, placing a selenite crystal on the floor just touching the top of your head at your crown chakra and a green aventurine crystal on your heart chakra. Feel the energy flow between the two stones along the midline of your body.

REMEDY #2: APACHE TEARS

Apache tears are excellent for easing sorrow and offering comfort. Carry Apache tears with you, as close to your heart as you can. For example, you may wish to tuck them into a shirt pocket or bra.

TIP: Connection to the Source, whatever you choose to call it (God, Buddha, Christ, Divine energy, Source, Goddess, and so on), can always provide comfort. Christians call this concept grace, in which the Divine source eases pain and sorrow. Permit yourself to connect to your Source, however you define it, through prayer or meditation in your moments of greatest sorrow, and allow the energy of the Divine to flow through you.

IMPROVED

Communication

Effective communication is important in developing and growing healthy and functional relationships. It can help you in your career, and it makes sharing your thoughts and ideas with others easier. While the throat chakra primarily controls personal truth and effective communication, you can be even more effective if you also seek higher guidance in communication via the crown chakra.

I clearly and calmly speak my truth.

MEDITATION

Amethyst works with your crown chakra to help you receive guidance and inspiration, which can help guide your words and communications, while lapis lazuli is a throat chakra stone that can help you clearly communicate. Sitting comfortably with your eyes closed, place an amethyst crystal on your crown chakra and hold a lapis lazuli crystal over your throat as you repeat the mantra for 10 minutes, or longer if you feel you need to.

REMEDY #1: ROSE QUARTZ & SODALITE

Speaking from a place of truth and love allows for effective communication. To bring love into your interactions, try this meditation. Lie on your back with a rose quartz crystal on your heart chakra and a sodalite crystal on your throat chakra. Close your eyes and repeat the mantra, "I communicate with love," for 10 minutes.

REMEDY #2: AQUAMARINE

Wear an aquamarine pendant around your neck or carry an aquamarine crystal in your pocket whenever communication is important. For example, use aquamarine when you have a presentation to make or an important job interview, or when you need to have an important conversation with a loved one.

 TIP: It's important to remember that communication is a two-way street, and listening is just as important as speaking. If you speak well but frequently miscommunicate because you don't listen well, working with blue throat chakra crystals can help improve this aspect of communication.

Compassion

Compassion is intricately linked to unconditional love, which is a function of the heart chakra. Compassion enables you to feel deeply for another and act toward them with kindness and care. Sometimes, compassion may be hard to find, particularly as it relates to difficult people in your life. However, responding with compassion toward others—even the most difficult people in your life—allows healing in your own life.

The spark of divinity in me recognizes the spark of divinity in you.

MEDITATION

Sit or lie comfortably with your eyes closed. Visualize the person for whom you wish to cultivate compassion. Now, as you repeat the mantra, visualize pure white light coming from your heart and entering the heart of that person, allowing the light to flow from both of you and surround you completely. Do this for about 10 minutes.

REMEDY #1: ROSE QUARTZ HEART CHAKRA WORK

Hold a piece of rose quartz in your receiving (nondominant) hand, pressing it gently against your heart chakra. Hold your giving (dominant) hand in front of you with your palm facing up. Close your eyes and imagine energy flowing from the crystal into your heart chakra, and then out through your giving hand and into the universe until it reaches the person for whom you wish to experience compassion. Perform this meditation for about 10 minutes.

REMEDY #2: CELESTITE

Celestite can help heal relationships and foster compassion. Carry a small piece of this beautiful light blue stone in your pocket when you are going to spend time with someone for whom you need to develop compassion.

 TIP: "The spark of divinity in me recognizes the spark of divinity in you" is the meaning of the word *namaste*. It is a reminder that everyone has the same spark of the Divine and that even though we seem different from one another, we are, in fact, all one. Meditating on your oneness with everyone on the planet can help you develop compassion for all—even the people who frustrate or anger you the most.

Confidence

Confidence comes from your solar plexus chakra, where you foster your sense of personal identity and self-esteem. Integrity, a heart chakra issue, also plays a role in confidence, because it is difficult to be confident when you are not living and speaking your truth. To grow more confident, pay close attention to these two chakras, learning who you are and then living that truth with integrity.

I exude confidence because I know I am living my truth.

MEDITATION

Sit or lie quietly with your eyes closed. Place a citrine crystal on your heart chakra and a lapis lazuli crystal on your throat chakra. Now, visualize yourself going about your day with the confidence that you are living within your integrity. Be as detailed in the visualization as possible. When you are done, repeat the mantra 10 times.

REMEDY #1: MOONSTONE

Wear moonstone jewelry or carry moonstone in your pocket whenever you need an extra boost of confidence. It is a stone that encourages you and provides strength for self-confidence.

REMEDY #2: HEMATITE

Hematite is a very powerful stone that helps build and boost self-confidence. Sleep with a piece of hematite under your pillow at night to help build your confidence while you sleep. When you awake in the morning, repeat the mantra 10 times before rising to go about your day.

Confusion

Life can be confusing sometimes. Whether it has an emotional, mental, spiritual, or physical cause, confusion can keep you stuck in the same place, which prevents you from progressing. Gaining clarity enables you to overcome the inertia caused by confusion, freeing you to move forward with your life in a positive and productive manner.

I see my life and choices clearly and move forward with self-assurance.

MEDITATION

Looking for guidance from your higher self and the Divine can help ease confusion and bring about clarity. Sit quietly with your eyes closed, breathing normally. Visualize a pure white light from above flowing into your crown chakra and bring the light down to your third eye chakra. Now, focus on your third eye, repeating the mantra for at least 10 minutes or until your confusion lifts.

REMEDY #1: AMETRINE

Ametrine can help increase clarity, which clears away confusion. It works with the third eye, helping you increase insight, as well as with the solar plexus chakra, which gives you confidence in your vision. When you are confused, carry ametrine in your pocket or wear it as a pendant around your neck. When you start to feel confused, hold the ametrine in your hand, close your eyes, and repeat the mantra 10 times, or until you feel a sense of peace.

REMEDY #2: SELENITE

Selenite is a high-vibration crystal that connects you to a higher source of wisdom. If you are experiencing confusion, hold a piece of selenite and sit or stand quietly for 5 to 10 minutes with your eyes closed, breathing deeply and repeating the mantra. You can also carry a piece of selenite with you throughout the day if you are experiencing ongoing confusion.

 TIP: If you often awaken feeling confused, sleep with a piece of ametrine or selenite under your pillow to help you gain clarity while you sleep.

Connection

WITH THE DIVINE

Within each of us lies a spark of the Divine. Every living creature and object on Earth is made up of the same energetic material, which comes directly from the Source. Connecting with the Divine serves many purposes, from balancing emotions to experiencing grace, gratitude, joy, and wonder. Taking the time to connect with the Divine daily through prayer or meditation can greatly enhance your life.

I welcome the presence of the Divine.
I exist within the Divine,
as the Divine exists within me.

MEDITATION

Sit quietly and comfortably, breathing normally. Ground and center yourself. Now, visualize a white light coming down from above and entering through your crown chakra. Allow the white light to flow through your body and out of you, completely filling and enveloping you. As you visualize, repeat the mantra. Sit within the white light for at least 10 minutes. Finish by grounding and centering again.

REMEDY #1: SUPER SEVEN

This is a very high-vibration crystal that contains seven different types of crystal within a single stone. It opens your aura and spirit to higher influence, while also awakening intuition. Use this powerful stone by holding it in your receiving (nondominant) hand during the meditation to aid in your connection to the Divine.

REMEDY #2: HERKIMER DIAMOND

The Herkimer diamond is another very powerful high-vibration crystal. Work with it in your meditation or prayer, holding it in your receiving (nondominant) hand as you meditate or pray.

 TIP: Because these crystals have such a high vibration, you will want to work with them in short spans, at least at first. Start by working with the crystals for 5 to 10 minutes, and work your way up to longer sessions of 30 to 60 minutes.

Connection

WITH ONE'S SPIRIT

Human beings are made up of mind, body, and spirit. Often, people are very good at connecting with one or two of those parts (usually mind and body), but not as effective at connecting with spirit. Connection with your spirit allows you to live in your integrity and walk the path your spirit intends, which is in alignment with your higher purpose.

I am grateful to my higher self, which guides me in all that I do.

MEDITATION

Sit comfortably with your eyes closed. Focus your attention inward, allowing yourself to travel to the place inside of you where your spirit dwells. As you focus your attention, repeat the mantra. Continue for at least 10 minutes.

REMEDY #1: RAINBOW FLUORITE

Because it works with all of your upper chakras, from your heart through your crown chakra, rainbow fluorite is very good at connecting you to your higher self. Place a rainbow fluorite under your pillow at night, repeating the mantra as you drift off to sleep. Keep a journal next to your bed to write down any insights you have upon awakening.

REMEDY #2: CELESTITE

Celestite can help you communicate with your higher self, as well. Hold a small piece in your receiving (nondominant) hand while you meditate, paying attention to any messages you receive.

 TIP: Your spirit is here to provide you with guidance. You can ask for guidance on specific issues. Try asking a question of your spirit as you drift off to sleep, and then record any dreams or insights you have when you awaken. Placing a piece of rainbow fluorite or celestite under your pillow may help amplify these messages. Receiving the information while you sleep can help remove anything, such as ego, that might block the information during your waking hours.

Contentment

Living a contented life means you are happy and at peace with your-self and your circumstances. Contentment doesn't mean stagnation, however. Instead, it is a conscious choice to remain peaceful in all circumstances. Picture contentment as the ability to remain peaceful in the midst of turmoil, sitting as still as a rock in a tornado, where the rock rests solidly on the ground while everything swirls in the tornado all around it.

I experience contentment and peace in all circumstances.

MEDITATION

Another way to visualize contentment is as a reed that bends in the wind, bending but never breaking, and then facing upright to the sun once the windstorm has passed. Sit quietly and comfortably, breathing normally. Repeat the mantra as you visualize a reed in heavy wind, always bending, never breaking, and always returning upright to face the sun. Do this for at least 10 minutes.

REMEDY #1: AMETHYST

Amethyst is a multipurpose stone, and it works especially well for establishing calm and contentment. Wear amethyst jewelry, such as a pendant or earrings, or carry a piece of amethyst in your pocket.

REMEDY #2: GREEN AVENTURINE HEART CHAKRA WORK

This stone imparts quiet contentment and tranquility, working with your heart chakra to add unconditional love. Lie on the floor with green aventurine on your heart chakra. Close your eyes and repeat the mantra for 10 minutes.

REMEDY #3: ROSE QUARTZ

This calm crystal of unconditional love can help you love your life and circumstances unconditionally, as well. Carry a piece of rose quartz in your pocket or keep one in a location where you spend a lot of time.

Courage

Having courage doesn't mean being unafraid. Rather, it means acting even in the face of fear. Some people require courage for small daily acts, while others require courage to make changes in their lives or face new situations. Regardless of why you need courage, finding the strength to act in ways that support your truth are essential to walking your spirit's path.

I give thanks to my higher self for giving me the courage to do everything I need to walk my spirit's path.

MEDITATION

Sit quietly in a comfortable position with your eyes closed. Repeat the mantra 10 times and visualize yourself performing whatever act it is you fear and coming through it with newfound strength. When you have completed your visualization, repeat the mantra 10 times again, or until you feel a sense of strength.

REMEDY #1: BLOODSTONE

Bloodstone is a crystal of the root and heart chakras, both of which are involved in the development of courage. The root chakra helps you overcome fear, while the heart chakra enables you to act with love and purpose. Meditate for 10 minutes holding your bloodstone in your receiving (nondominant) hand while you repeat the mantra.

REMEDY #2: SNOWFLAKE OBSIDIAN

A root chakra stone, snowflake obsidian helps ground you and enables you to overcome fear so you can take action. Carry snowflake obsidian in your pocket whenever you need extra courage.

REMEDY #3: CARNELIAN

Another stone of the root and sacral chakras, carnelian allows you to focus on achieving what you need to, no matter how much you fear it. It's a great stone to have in your pocket while you're trying to gain the courage to ask for a raise or promotion at work.

Creativity

Human beings are naturally creative, because we get to create who and what we are each and every day. Sometimes, however, we get stuck in a rut and our creativity seems to dry up. Creativity is a sacral chakra issue, so working with sacral chakra stones like carnelian can help spark creativity.

I give thanks to the universe for providing me with an unlimited source of creativity.

MEDITATION

Holding a carnelian stone, sit quietly with your eyes closed and your attention focused on your sacral chakra. As you inhale, imagine creativity flowing from the universe in through your sacral chakra. As you exhale, imagine the creativity flowing from your sacral chakra throughout your body. As you breathe, repeat the mantra 10 times, or until you feel a sense of peace.

REMEDY #1: AMETRINE

Ametrine is a naturally occurring gemstone that is a combination of two creativity-inducing crystals, amethyst and citrine. To spark creativity, tape an ametrine crystal to the bottom of your office chair. For inspiration while you sleep, place an ametrine crystal under your pillow.

REMEDY #2: IOLITE

Iolite, also known as water sapphire, is a powerful creativity booster, and it can help spark inspiration. Wear iolite jewelry or carry a piece of iolite in your pocket whenever you need a little extra inspiration.

 TIP: If you work in a creative profession, such as writing or graphic design, place a bowl of gemstone beads made from creative crystals like ametrine and chalcedony on your desk.

Denial

Denial is a way of lying to ourselves, although we don't do it with bad intent. Rather, it is how our ego protects us from information that, on a subconscious level, we feel may harm us. While denial is a self-protective mechanism, it is almost never constructive. Pushing past denial and looking at the reality of a situation is the only way we can effectively move through and past it.

I see all aspects of my life and self clearly and with compassion.

MEDITATION

Stand in front of a mirror and gaze deeply into your eyes. Start by stating the mantra and affirming love, kindness, and compassion for yourself. Next, speak whatever you have been denying aloud, but with kindness, maintaining eye contact with yourself in the mirror the entire time. Gaze into your own eyes for five minutes, repeating the mantra. When you finish, ground and center yourself, and visualize yourself surrounded by a pure, white, loving light.

REMEDY #1: RAINBOW FLUORITE

Rainbow fluorite works with multiple chakras simultaneously because it has multiple colors. In this case, the purple in the fluorite helps you gain spiritual insight via your third eye chakra, the blue helps you live within your truth via the throat chakra, and the green works with the heart chakra to help you view yourself compassionately. All are important in overcoming denial. Hold a piece of rainbow fluorite in your receiving (nondominant) hand while you complete the meditation, or carry it with you in a pocket as you go about your day.

REMEDY #2: RHODOCHROSITE

Rhodochrosite is a gemstone that removes the blockages causing denial. Sleep with it under your pillow at night, and write down any realizations you have in a journal in the morning. Then, visualize yourself surrounded by a loving and healing white light.

 TIP: If someone in your life is experiencing denial about a problem such as an addiction, give that person a piece of rhodochrosite or rainbow fluorite to help see things more clearly.

Depression

Everyone feels a bit blue from time to time, but when that sadness persists, it may grow into chronic depression. Depression can affect your mind, body, and spirit, causing lingering physical pain and ennui that keeps you from living a vibrant, joyful, and productive life. If you are experiencing short-term or long-term depression, try these remedies in conjunction with professional therapy.

I seek out and enjoy all the pleasure and happiness available to me in my daily life.

MEDITATION

Gratitude is an excellent way to help you find the small joys in your life. Sit quietly with your eyes closed. Speak the mantra aloud, and then say, "I am grateful for . . . ." State something large or small that brings you peace and joy. Repeat this for as many things as you can find for which you are grateful. Finish by repeating the mantra.

REMEDY #1: AMBER

Amber is a happy crystal that can help elevate your mood. Wear amber jewelry whenever you need a boost.

REMEDY #2: CLEAR QUARTZ GRID

Clear quartz is a great all-purpose crystal for mental, emotional, and spiritual healing. It can help ease many of the issues associated with depression. Make a simple circular grid with eight clear quartz points and a larger piece of clear quartz in the center, aiming the points away from the center stone to direct the energy out into the room. Place it near where you sleep or work.

REMEDY #3: SMOKY QUARTZ

Smoky quartz absorbs negative energy and replaces it with positive energy. Keep smoky quartz with you at all times, wearing it as jewelry or carrying it in your pocket. Be sure to cleanse the crystals daily, especially if you have severe depression.

Despair

Despair occurs when you have lost all hope. When you are in despair, it may feel dark and difficult to function. It robs you of motivation and leaves you feeling empty and alone. The way to combat despair is to begin to reconnect with anything that makes you feel hopeful, no matter how small or insignificant it might seem. Once you can allow hope to reenter, you are on your way to healing. Despair is a very serious emotional situation that may require mental health care, as well. If you are contemplating self-harm, please seek professional guidance.

For everything that ends, there is a new beginning. I welcome my new beginning with gratitude.

MEDITATION

Instead of sitting and quietly meditating, seek out beauty. Visit someplace that you feel is exceptionally beautiful and spend time there, or listen to a piece of music that you love. Repeat the mantra for at least 10 minutes as you experience the beauty.

REMEDY #1: SMOKY QUARTZ

Despair is a very negative emotion. Smoky quartz can help absorb the negativity and turn it into positive energy. Sleep with smoky quartz under your pillow and carry it with you wherever you go, cleansing the crystals daily.

REMEDY #2: CELESTITE

Celestite can help awaken hope. When you are in deepest despair, always carry celestite with you in your pocket. Cleanse it daily.

REMEDY #3: PINK CALCITE

Pink calcite can help you find hope in the midst of despair, while reminding you of unconditional love. Sleep with pink calcite under your pillow.

Discernment

Discernment gives you the ability to judge situations well and make good choices. It is necessary for wisdom. Proper discernment comes from your higher self and is an intuitive process. Tuning in to the messages from your soul as well as the Divine, which are third eye and crown chakra abilities, can improve your discernment so you can make choices that serve your life's path.

I can clearly see the truth in any situation, and I make good choices as a result.

MEDITATION

Practice mindfulness meditation to improve discernment. Sit quietly and notice your breathing without trying to control it. As thoughts arise, notice them and allow them to drift away naturally without trying to control them. Do this for 10 minutes, then repeat the mantra 10 times.

REMEDY #1: QUARTZ & AMETHYST CHAKRA WORK

Lie on your back. Place a clear quartz crystal on the floor, just touching your crown chakra, and place an amethyst crystal on your third eye chakra. Repeat the mantra for about 10 minutes and feel the energy flow into your crown chakra and to your third eye chakra.

REMEDY #2: IOLITE

Iolite is a third eye chakra crystal that brings insight and helps you turn it into wisdom. Iolite is a very beautiful crystal in jewelry, so if you can find an iolite necklace or earrings, wear these. Otherwise, place iolite under your pillow at night. Repeat the mantra as you drift off to sleep. Keep a journal next to the bed and write down any insights upon waking.

 TIP: If you're struggling with an issue requiring discernment or wisdom, carry the clear quartz and amethyst you use for meditation with you throughout the day. Always keep a piece of scratch paper or a journal handy to write down any insights that arise, and read them later when you aren't busy.

Eating Disorders

While on the surface, eating disorders appear to be about food, they tend to have spiritual, mental, and emotional roots. Because of the immediate threat to your physical health, it is important to seek the help of a qualified medical professional when dealing with an eating disorder. However, these remedies and meditations can provide a source of complementary therapy.

My body, mind, and spirit are beautiful, and I bless myself with unconditional love.

MEDITATION

Anytime you feel compulsive behaviors associated with your eating disorder arising, stop for a moment before you act. Close your eyes, place both hands gently over your heart chakra, and take three deep, full breaths. Picture white light entering your body through your crown chakra and surrounding you completely as you repeat the mantra. Do this until the urge passes.

REMEDY #1: ROSE QUARTZ

Since eating disorders are often about a lack of self-love, carrying a rose quartz crystal near your heart (in a shirt pocket or bra) can help you find unconditional self-love. When you feel the urge to engage in a compulsive behavior related to your eating disorder, hold the rose quartz in your hands over your heart chakra as you do the meditation.

REMEDY #2: CARNELIAN

Carnelian is a stone that fosters self-acceptance and helps with motivation. Keeping carnelian with you always—in a pocket during the day and under your pillow at night—can help with your recovery process.

 TIP: Because the energy associated with eating disorders tends to be very powerful, cleanse and recharge any stones you use daily. It may help to have several stones in rotation so you always have a cleansed and charged stone ready to go.

Emotional Balance

When your life gets out of balance, things often start to go wrong. Maintaining emotional balance helps you stay steady throughout the day, which allows you to think clearly, access your creativity, experience gratitude, and enjoy your life. While you may experience emotional lows and highs throughout the course of your life, maintaining emotional balance enables you to always return to your center.

I allow my emotions to serve as opportunities for growth, and then I return to my center.

MEDITATION

Daily mindfulness meditation practice can help you balance your emotions. Sit quietly and notice your breath without trying to control it. As thoughts and emotions arise, notice them as an observer but don't get caught up in them. Instead, allow them to pass by quickly. Meditate for at least 10 minutes first thing in the morning.

REMEDY #1: GARNET ROOT CHAKRA MEDITATION

Your root chakra is the foundation of your emotional health, according to medical intuitive Caroline Myss. Meditate holding a garnet in your receiving (nondominant) hand, focusing on your root chakra, to create a stable foundation for your emotions.

REMEDY #2: MALACHITE

Malachite is a heart chakra stone that helps rebalance that chakra. Wearing a malachite necklace, bracelet, or ring can help rebalance emotional energy coming from the heart.

REMEDY #3: RAINBOW FLUORITE

The many colors in rainbow fluorite work with your higher chakras, from the heart to the third eye, creating balance among them, which can help balance your emotions. Carry rainbow fluorite in your pocket, or wear a rainbow fluorite necklace or earrings.

Emotional Blockage

Blocked or trapped emotions can prevent a free flow of energy between your chakras and throughout your body. When energy is blocked in this way, it can affect all aspects of your health: mental, physical, emotional, and spiritual. You may experience blocked emotions as physical symptoms, or you may experience a sensation of mental, emotional, or spiritual numbness. Releasing these blockages is important for living a life of joy and purpose.

I experience each emotion fully and then release it into the universe.

MEDITATION

Sit or lie comfortably. Close your eyes and mentally scan your body. Visualize anywhere that feels blocked or congested as a dark shadow. Shine a white light on the shadow and watch as the light breaks it up, lifting the shadow up and out of your body as it dissolves into the universe. Repeat the mantra as you release each blockage.

REMEDY #1: AMETHYST

Amethyst can help facilitate emotional release. Hold an amethyst in your receiving (nondominant) hand as you perform the meditation.

REMEDY #2: CLEAR QUARTZ GRID

Set up a simple square grid with five pieces of clear quartz of any shape. Put the largest piece in the center, and then set up four pieces around it, making four corners of a box. Place the grid near your meditation space.

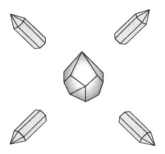

REMEDY #3: LAPIS LAZULI

Wear a lapis lazuli pendant around your neck. Lapis can help release blocked emotions and foster self-acceptance.

Emotional Trauma

When you've experienced an emotional trauma, it may be difficult to regain your emotional footing. Emotional trauma can affect you long after the event has passed, causing posttraumatic stress that remains buried deeply in your subconscious, waiting to pop back into your conscious mind. Dealing with the trauma as quickly as possible can help you move through it, so it doesn't cause you future pain. If you are experiencing posttraumatic stress disorder (PTSD), please seek help from a qualified professional.

I release the past because it cannot be changed, and I now choose healing.

MEDITATION

Sit comfortably with your eyes closed, breathing normally. Repeat the mantra for at least 10 minutes, allowing any feelings you have to arise. As feelings of emotional trauma arise, visualize them surrounded in white light, which lifts them away from you and into the universe. Finish the meditation by affirming, "I give thanks to the universal healing light for lifting away my negative emotions."

REMEDY #1: ROSE QUARTZ HEART CHAKRA WORK

Unconditional self-love is an important part of making your way through emotional trauma. Lie on your back with a piece of rose quartz on your heart chakra for 10 minutes, allowing the feelings of unconditional love to wash over you.

REMEDY #2: BLACK TOURMALINE

Emotional trauma often results in negative vibrations. Carry a piece of black tourmaline in your pocket at all times to absorb these negative vibrations as they arise from you, removing them from your body.

 TIP: Because emotional trauma can have such heavy energy, it's important to cleanse and recharge the crystals you use to overcome trauma daily, keeping a few crystals in rotation so you always have a fresh one with you.

Empathy

Empathy enables you to understand and share another person's feelings. It is an important part of developing kindness and relating to and forming relationships with others. It is possible, however, to be overly empathetic and take on other people's feelings as your own, so it is important to find ways to protect yourself against overempathizing.

I am one with all that is.

MEDITATION

Using a oneness meditation to realize your connection with others can help you develop empathy. Sit comfortably and close your eyes. Breathe normally and say the mantra aloud. Focus your attention within, and then push it outward, expanding beyond your body and into the universe. As your energy and focus expands, notice that you can no longer tell where your energy leaves off and another's begins. Repeat the mantra for at least 10 minutes.

REMEDY #1: BLUE ARAGONITE

Use blue aragonite to increase empathy with others. Whenever you struggle with empathy for another person, carry blue aragonite with you when you will interact with that person, to help foster this emotion.

REMEDY #2: BLACK TOURMALINE

If you are an overempathizer, you can use black tourmaline to absorb excess energy. Overempathizers can wear black tourmaline around the neck or carry it in a pocket.

 TIP: When you take on the emotions of another and overempathize, close your eyes. Visualize two volume switches in your head: one labeled "me" and the other labeled "everyone else." Turn the "me" switch all the way up, and turn down the "everyone else" switch to a low level.

Empowerment

When you are empowered, you feel able to take on the world and achieve the things necessary to walk your life's path. Living in modern society often leaves us feeling drained of our empowerment, making us feel marginalized or unable to complete important tasks. Reclaiming your sense of empowerment is an important step for living in joy and integrity.

I have a Divine spark in me, and it empowers me to live the life I choose.

MEDITATION

Close your eyes and sit comfortably, breathing normally. Say the mantra aloud. Then, visualize doing the things you need to do to move your life forward with confidence, following each to its logical outcome. When you are done visualizing, say, "I give thanks to my higher self for granting me the empowerment to follow my soul's path."

REMEDY #1: SUNSTONE CHAKRA WORK

Sunstone is a sacral chakra stone, which is where your personal power is formed. Lie on your back with a sunstone on your sacral chakra. Visualize orange light swirling within your chakra, radiating outward into the universe.

REMEDY #2: CARNELIAN & CLEAR QUARTZ GRID

Make a simple grid from one large carnelian stone of any shape and eight clear quartz points. Place the carnelian in the center, and place each of the quartz points in a circle around the stone with the points facing outward. The quartz will amplify the empowerment from the carnelian, directing it into the surrounding area. Keep the grid near the area where you spend most of your time.

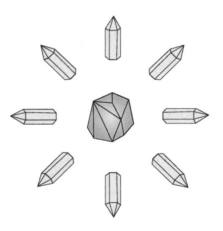

 TIP: Some people mistake empowerment for license to do whatever they want, no matter who it hurts. Remember that true empowerment comes with responsibility. You still need to act in a kind and compassionate manner toward others as you follow your path.

Faith

Faith can take many forms. For some, faith means an unwavering belief in a higher power. For others, faith is about trust in a benevolent universe. Others may believe the only faith that matters is faith in yourself and others. Still, for most people, faith (or lack thereof) plays some type of role in their lives. Whatever it is you need to develop faith in, these remedies can help.

I have faith that I have everything I need to follow my path.

MEDITATION

Faith comes more naturally as you develop trust, and expressing gratitude as your trust is fulfilled can help you grow in your faith. This is a living meditation you can perform throughout the day to remind you that your faith is justified. In the morning, before rising, speak the mantra aloud. Then, as you go through your day, whenever something good comes to you from the universe, no matter how small, take a moment to silently express your gratitude.

REMEDY #1: MOONSTONE

Moonstone is a higher vibrational stone that connects us to whatever higher power we believe in. Wearing it as a necklace or carrying moonstone in your pocket can help you develop or strengthen your own faith.

REMEDY #2: LABRADORITE

This crystal flashes with many colors, so it works with many of your chakras. It's also a high-vibration stone that helps connect you to a higher power, which can strengthen your faith. Place a piece of labradorite under your pillow at night. As you drift off to sleep, repeat the mantra. Then, upon waking, repeat the mantra at least 10 times.

REMEDY #3: SELENITE CROWN CHAKRA WORK

Lie on your back on the floor, with your eyes closed. Place a piece of selenite on the floor above your head so it touches your crown chakra. Stay in this position for 10 minutes as you repeat the mantra.

Fear

Fear is an instinctive survival response possessed by all living creatures. Sometimes, fear can save your life because it activates the fight-or-flight response. However, generalized fear/anxiety or ongoing fear related to issues that are not life-threatening can cause you to become paralyzed and keep you from following your soul's path.

I follow my soul's path fearlessly.

MEDITATION

Sit comfortably and close your eyes. Speak the mantra. Now, ask yourself, "What do I fear?" Focus on your root chakra and pay attention to the answer that arises. When you know what it is you fear, picture the fear as a solid object, lifting away from your body and dissolving into the atmosphere. Repeat the mantra. Then ask, "What do I fear?" again. Repeat the process until no fears come up.

REMEDY #1: BLACK TOURMALINE

Fear comes from the root chakra, which deals with issues of safety and security. Black tourmaline is an excellent root chakra stone, and it also absorbs negative energy. Use black tourmaline on your root chakra during the meditation. If you remain fearful, carry a piece of black tourmaline in your pocket throughout the day. Be sure to cleanse the crystal daily.

REMEDY #2: RED SPINEL

Red spinel is another good root chakra stone. Use the spinel in a salt bath. Fill a tub with warm water, swirling in about ¼ cup of Himalayan pink salt or sea salt. Get in the tub, and add a piece of spinel to the water. Soak for 15 minutes. Remove the spinel from the tub and pull the drain plug. Allow the water to drain completely, carrying away your fears, before you get out of the tub. Be sure to cleanse your crystal before using it again.

Forgiveness

Many people misunderstand forgiveness, thinking it is for the person they are forgiving instead of for themselves. In fact, forgiveness is all about you. It's a way of saying, "I no longer choose to allow your actions to affect my life." Failing to forgive another can lock you into negativity, keeping you from moving forward on your life's path. Choosing to forgive, on the other hand, can set you free from the burden of the harm of others.

I forgive anyone who has caused me harm and release that person into a positive future.

MEDITATION

Sit quietly with your eyes closed. Visualize the person you need to forgive and speak the mantra. Surround the person with white, healing light, saying, "I thank you for the role you have played in my life." Now, list any positive effects, no matter how small, the person's actions may have helped bring about in your life. Finally, say, "I forgive you and release you into a positive future."

REMEDY #1: RHODOCHROSITE HEART CHAKRA WORK

Forgiveness is a function of the heart chakra. Rhodochrosite stimulates the heart chakra, enabling you to forgive with kindness, compassion, and unconditional love. Lie on your back with rhodochrosite on your heart chakra, repeating the mantra for 10 minutes or until you feel forgiveness.

REMEDY #2: APACHE TEARS

Apache tears can help dissolve negativity toward yourself and others. Hold these crystals in your receiving (nondominant) hand while you meditate. You can also carry them in your pocket when you know you will be coming into contact with a person you need to forgive.

REMEDY #3: PERIDOT

If it's yourself you need to forgive, wear the gemstone peridot as a pendant around your neck. Peridot can help you face your own issues with honesty while allowing you to forgive yourself for your choices and actions.

ACHIEVING

Goals

Setting and achieving goals is an important part of our path. Sometimes when we're pursuing long-term goals, however, we get discouraged at how long it is taking and lose motivation. It's important to remember that, while walking a straight line to a goal may seem ideal, sometimes the detours on the ways to our goals offer the most valuable lessons and insights.

Anything blocking my path to my goals dissolves in this moment.

MEDITATION

One of the best ways to achieve your goals in meditation is through visualization. Sit comfortably with your eyes closed, breathing normally. Speak the mantra. Now, visualize yourself living your life when you have achieved your goal. What will your life look like? What will you do? How will you feel? Make your visualization as detailed as you can. Finish by speaking the mantra again.

REMEDY #1: CARNELIAN

One of the things that often prevents us from achieving our goals is fear, which causes inaction. Fear is a root chakra issue, and carnelian can help unblock this chakra. Carry a piece of carnelian in your pants pocket to help spur you toward goal-oriented action.

REMEDY #2: CLEAR QUARTZ & AFFIRMATIONS

You can use the Law of Attraction to achieve your goals. Basically, the Law of Attraction states that you attract what you focus your energy on. Therefore, if you change your thoughts about a thing, you'll change how it manifests in your life. You can use clear quartz to amplify this. Create positively spoken affirmations for each of your goals. Then, repeat them daily as you hold a piece of clear quartz in either or both hands for amplification.

 TIP: When you create affirmations, it is important to choose positive statements over negative ones. If you use a negative statement, the Law of Attraction will deliver the negative. So, instead of an affirmation that says, "I'm not broke anymore," word it in a positive way, such as, "I have all the money I need to live a comfortable life." It's also essential to eliminate negative thoughts from your mind as much as possible and to take action toward your goals. When you catch yourself thinking a negative thought, immediately cancel it and replace it with a positive statement.

Gratitude

When we live our lives with gratitude, we develop an appreciation for the things we have. This gratitude allows us to focus on the positive in our lives, which creates an energy by which more positivity comes to us. Sometimes, circumstances make it difficult to feel grateful. In those times, you can still cultivate gratitude by focusing on small things for which to be grateful, even if it's something as simple as, "I'm grateful I had clean water to drink today."

I am grateful to the Source for all the good in my life.

MEDITATION

Every day, spend at least 10 minutes meditating on all the things for which you are grateful. Close your eyes and speak the mantra. Then, for each thing, say, "I am grateful for [name the thing]."

REMEDY #1: ANGELITE

Angelite is a crystal that fosters gratitude. If you need to cultivate gratitude, carry a piece of this serene blue stone in your pocket.

REMEDY #2: CLEAR QUARTZ PRAYER BEADS

Clear quartz serves as an amplifier. It also opens up communication to a higher source. When you wish to amplify your gratitude and send it out into the universe, use a beaded clear quartz necklace or bracelet as a form of prayer beads. As you finger each bead, list one thing for which you are grateful, beginning and ending with the mantra.

Grief

Grief is an inevitable part of the human experience. It is part of the duality in which we exist. Without grief, we wouldn't be able to recognize or appreciate joy. But that knowledge doesn't make grief any easier. When you experience a tragic or sad event, it is necessary to allow yourself to grieve. It's equally important that you don't get so caught up in the grief that you can't emerge on the other side to enjoy life once again.

I turn to the Divine for comfort during my time of grief.

MEDITATION

Sit quietly with your eyes closed, breathing normally. Speak the mantra. Allow yourself to feel your emotions as they arise. Do not block them, but allow them to fully form. Once the emotion has lessened, visualize a white light coming down from above and enveloping you in a warm, healing white glow. Continue your meditation for at least 10 minutes.

REMEDY #1: OBSIDIAN

Grief is a very powerful emotion. One stone that can absorb some of your grief is black obsidian. During times of extreme grief, carry black obsidian in your pants pocket, taking care to cleanse and recharge it daily.

REMEDY #2: SMOKY QUARTZ

Smoky quartz will turn negative energy into positive energy. Sit quietly, holding the smoky quartz in your receiving (nondominant) hand as you repeat the mantra. Allow the grief to flow naturally. Continue until the grief lessens. Repeat this as often as you need to during your time of grieving.

 TIP: Many people believe there is a time limit on grieving. There isn't. It's important to honor how you feel and allow yourself to fully experience the grief, no matter how painful it is. These tools won't stop the grief, but they can help keep you from getting so stuck in the grief that you descend into depression.

Grounding

Grounding keeps us connected to the Earth, which is our source of support and strength. Daily grounding can help keep you focused and centered. Ground whenever you feel out of sorts, if you're dizzy or confused, or if you're just not feeling quite right. It is also important to ground after meditation, prayer, or other spiritual or cerebral activities.

I honor the jewel within the lotus bloom.
(Om mani padme hum.)

MEDITATION

Om mani padme hum (pronounced *ohm mah-nee pahd-may hum*) is a Sanskrit mantra often used for grounding and centering. The lotus represents spiritual birth or development, while the jewel represents humans' divinity living within spirituality. This is the perfect mantra to use with a simple mantra meditation. Sit comfortably holding any of the grounding stones listed in this section in either hand. Breathe normally and repeat the mantra softly out loud or to yourself for at least 10 minutes, or longer if needed.

REMEDY #1: LODESTONE GROUNDING VISUALIZATION

Sit in a comfortable position on the floor where you are unlikely to be disturbed. Clasp a lodestone gently between your hands, which are placed in your lap. Close your eyes. Visualize yourself dropping roots from your core and extending into the Earth, wrapping themselves around the Earth's core. Continue your meditation for at least 10 minutes.

REMEDY #2: BLACK TOURMALINE

Hold black tourmaline in your receiving (nondominant) hand. Remove your shoes and step outside onto the grass in bare feet. Close your eyes for about 10 minutes and feel your connection to the Earth below you.

REMEDY #3: OBSIDIAN

For help staying grounded, carry a piece of obsidian in your pocket.

Hope

Hope is necessary to keep humans moving forward. In the absence of hope, we lose the motivation to take action or improve our circumstances. Complete loss of hope can lead to despair or despondency. Sometimes it may feel difficult to keep hope alive. Fostering hope, even in dark times, can help pull you through.

My hope that good things will happen in my life, today and every day, is alive.

MEDITATION

List five things you'd like to manifest in your life. Now, write those five things in the form of affirmations, using positive statements as if you already have them. For example, "I am grateful that I have earned my master's degree." Now, look at yourself in the mirror, making eye contact, and repeat each affirmation five times.

REMEDY #1: CLEAR QUARTZ

Hold a piece of clear quartz in your receiving (nondominant) hand as you complete the meditation. The quartz will amplify your affirmations and help connect you with the Source.

REMEDY #2: SELENITE

Selenite is a high-vibration crystal that can help connect you with hope. Place a piece of selenite on your beside table. As you drift off to sleep, repeat the mantra. When you wake up in the morning, repeat the mantra again 10 times.

REMEDY #3: AMAZONITE

Known as the hope stone, amazonite can help you focus on hopefulness instead of despair. I use amazonite as a worry stone, holding it in my hand and rubbing its smooth surface with my thumb. Carry a piece in your pocket, and rub it whenever you feel you need an infusion of hope.

Indecisiveness

Life would be so much easier if we were decisive every moment of every day. Some decisions may seem more difficult than others to make, however. When I make my decisions, I tend to be very intuition-based (as opposed to logic-based, much to my very logical husband's consternation). This typically serves me quite well. Still, even with the power of intuition guiding me, sometimes I get stuck and have difficulty making a choice. When you have difficult decisions to make and you can't tell what your gut wants you to do, try these remedies.

I am in tune with what I need, and I trust my intuition to guide me to the right choices.

MEDITATION

Sit or lie comfortably with your eyes closed. Focus your attention on your third eye chakra as you consider the decision you need to make. Pay attention to any images or information you receive. Do this for at least 10 minutes or until you have reached a comfortable decision.

REMEDY #1: AMETHYST

As you perform the meditation, hold an amethyst, which is a highly intuitive gemstone, in your receiving (nondominant) hand, paying close attention to any perceptions that arise.

REMEDY #2: AMETRINE

Ametrine works well because it combines amethyst and citrine. Amethyst will help you with your intuitive problem solving, while citrine will help you determine what you want, as it is a solar plexus chakra stone tied to self-identity. When you have a big decision to make, carry a piece of ametrine in your pocket.

 TIP: If you don't have ametrine, don't worry. You can also carry a piece of natural citrine and a piece of amethyst together in your pocket for the same effect.

Insecurity

Insecurity may be an issue with the solar plexus chakra, which is associated with self-confidence. It may also stem from the root chakra, where we develop our feelings of safety and security. Feeling insecure may undermine you, because it causes negative thought patterns that disrupt any affirmative work you are trying to do. Finding a way to lessen or release insecurity is a necessary step in following your path.

I believe in my ability to accomplish anything I set out to do.

MEDITATION

Sit comfortably with both hands placed gently over your solar plexus chakra. Close your eyes and breathe normally. Visualize your solar plexus chakra filling with a golden yellow light. As you do, repeat the mantra. Continue for at least 10 minutes, or perform this visualization for a minute or two whenever you are feeling insecure.

REMEDY #1: YELLOW TIGERS EYE

This is a solar plexus chakra stone of confidence. Hold a piece of yellow tigers eye over your solar plexus chakra as you perform the meditation. You can also wear yellow tigers eye as a pendant or carry a stone in your pocket whenever you are feeling insecure.

REMEDY #2: CARNELIAN ROOT CHAKRA WORK

If your insecurity is related to safety, security, or family issues, this meditation can help strengthen the root chakra, where you develop your sense of safety and security. Lie on your back with a carnelian on your root chakra. Close your eyes and visualize red swirling light in the area of the chakra. Repeat the mantra "I am grateful to be safe and secure," for at least 10 minutes.

REMEDY #3: BLACK TOURMALINE

If you feel psychically unsafe, use black tourmaline to protect you, carrying it in your pocket or wearing it as a pendant around your neck. The tourmaline absorbs any negative psychic energy around you, protecting you. Be sure to cleanse the tourmaline after every use.

Insomnia/ Sleeplessness

Many factors can contribute to the sleep disorder insomnia, such as stress, physical pain, inconsistent sleep patterns, and environmental issues, such as being too warm or too cold. If you're like most people, you need a decent night of sleep (between seven and nine hours) to function well. Along with adjusting any factors that may keep you from sleeping well, such as ambient light or uncomfortable room temperature, try these remedies to help you get a full night of sleep.

I release the stress of my day and drift off into deep, refreshing sleep.

MEDITATION

At bedtime, use progressive relaxation and mindfulness to clear your mind of stressful thoughts and promote relaxation and restfulness in your body. Lie on your back with your eyes closed. Breathe deeply but naturally. Starting with your feet, with each exhalation, imagine all of the tension draining out of that body part, leaving it completely relaxed. Work your way from your feet all the way to your head, one body part at a time. If thoughts arise as you do this, notice them but then watch them drift away. Do not get stuck in any single thought or thought pattern. Acknowledge the thought and let it go. After you reach your head, rest peacefully until you drift off to sleep.

REMEDY #1: AMETHYST

Amethyst is a powerful crystal, which many people use for insomnia. Start with a newly cleansed and charged piece of amethyst. About an hour before going to bed, stop using any backlit screens, such as tablets, computers, or smartphones. Turn on soft, relaxing music and begin your bedtime routine. Engage in a quiet activity such as reading for about 20 minutes. Next, run a warm bath and add Epsom salts. Soak for 10 minutes and then dry yourself off. Now, sit quietly in a very dimly lit room, holding your charged amethyst in your receiving (non-dominant) hand. Breathe deeply. With each exhalation, repeat the word "relax" to yourself. Continue for 10 minutes. Now, crawl into bed and place the amethyst under your pillow. If you're still having trouble sleeping, complete the progressive relaxation technique described in the meditation.

REMEDY #2: MOONSTONE

Moonstone is another crystal that aids relaxation and facilitates deep sleep. Place a piece of moonstone on your bedside table to help you get some shut-eye.

Inspiration

Sometimes you just need a little inspiration. While many people think of inspiration in terms of creative pursuits, it can really apply to any aspect of your life. For example, you may need inspiration to solve a problem in a relationship, or you may require some help to determine the next step you are taking in your life. Whatever type of inspiration you need, it comes to you from two places—your higher self and the Source—making it an issue of the third eye and crown chakras.

I give thanks to the Source for daily inspiration to walk my life's path.

MEDITATION

Sit quietly and comfortably with your eyes closed, breathing normally. Visualize light flowing into your crown chakra from the universe. As you visualize, repeat the mantra several times. Do this for at least 10 minutes.

REMEDY #1: AMETHYST

Amethyst is the perfect crystal for inspiration. It stimulates both the third eye and crown chakras, so it is wonderful for awakening insight and providing inspiration. If you are trying to find inspiration for a certain issue, sleep on it. Hold an amethyst crystal in your hand and perform the meditation before you go to bed. Now, place the amethyst crystal under your pillow. As you drift off to sleep, repeat the mantra, "I give thanks to the Source for providing me with inspiration about [fill in the blank]." Keep a notebook next to your bed, and write down any inspiration or ideas you have upon waking.

REMEDY #2: SUPER SEVEN

If you work in a field that requires creative problem-solving, keep a piece of super seven at your desk. When you need a boost of inspiration, sit quietly with the crystal in your receiving (nondominant) hand while breathing deeply for one minute.

 TIP: Dreams can serve as a powerful source of inspiration. Ask for inspiration for any issue you are facing before you go to sleep, and then diligently record your dreams upon waking. Look for patterns or symbols in the dreams that inspire you to take action.

Intuition

Intuition comes from your third eye chakra, which is the center of insight. All humans are intuitive, but many of us have stopped listening to our intuition, relying solely on logic to make decisions. When we ignore our intuition, it tends to grow less active. In my experience, when I struggle between making a logical choice and an intuitive choice, I discover that the intuitive choice is the one that truly helps me get where I want and need to go.

I listen to and trust my intuition as my source of guidance.

MEDITATION

Sit or lie comfortably with your eyes closed. Focus all your attention on your third eye chakra, paying attention to any images, thoughts, sounds, or symbols that appear. Do this for at least 10 minutes. Write down your impressions after your meditation.

REMEDY #1: CELESTITE THIRD EYE CHAKRA WORK

Lie on your back comfortably with a piece of celestite placed directly on your third eye chakra. Close your eyes and repeat the mantra 10 times. Now, ask a question about something for which you are seeking inspiration. Pay close attention to the images, thoughts, sounds, or symbols that arise.

REMEDY #2: AMETHYST

When you feel you really need intuitive help, carry a newly cleansed and charged piece of amethyst in your pocket. Several times through-out the day, hold the amethyst in your receiving (nondominant) hand, paying close attention to anything that arises.

 TIP: Many people think intuitive thought has to take a specific form, such as images or voices. However, different people receive intuition in different ways. For some, it may be a sudden knowing or an idea that appears fully formed. For others, intuition arises via symbolic or nonsymbolic images they see with their mind's eye. Other people may have physical sensations in their body, hear a voice talking to them, have a dream, or have an unusually persistent thought. All of these are valid forms of intuition, so it's important to pay close attention to how you receive and process information.

Irritability

It would be wonderful if we could all go through life in a state of happiness and bliss, but most of us don't. It's perfectly natural to get a little irritable from time to time. Many factors in life can contribute to irritability, such as stress, lack of sleep, hormonal changes, dietary issues, or even atmospheric conditions. Crystals can help even out your mood, allowing you to be more even-keeled as you seek out the root of why you're feeling so irritable.

I am calm, peaceful, and even-tempered.

MEDITATION

Sit or lie comfortably with your eyes closed, breathing normally. As you breathe, repeat the mantra. Pay close attention to your body and notice where your irritability takes a physical toll in the form of clenched muscles, aches and pains, or other physical sensations. As you focus on each area, repeat the mantra and surround that area in a beautiful green light for at least 10 minutes, or until the discomfort dissipates.

REMEDY #1: GREEN JADE

Green jade is soothing and calming. It is a stone of unconditional love and acceptance. Wear a green jade pendant or carry green jade close to your heart when you are feeling irritable. If the irritability threatens to erupt, hold the jade in your receiving (nondominant) hand as you breathe deeply until it passes.

REMEDY #2: PERIDOT HEART CHAKRA WORK

Peridot is a stone that works with your heart chakra, enabling you to act with love in difficult situations. If you awake in the morning feeling irritable, lie quietly with peridot on your heart chakra and repeat the mantra for 10 minutes before you go about your day.

Joy & Happiness

When you ask people what they want in life, many are likely to answer that they just want to be happy. While many people desire happiness, a large number don't have any idea how to find it or sustain it. Joy arises from focusing on the moment, paying attention to the small things that bring us pleasure and peace in life. If you can remain focused on the present throughout your day, it is easier to find joy in the journey.

I focus on the now, and I notice and appreciate the joy that small things bring into my life.

MEDITATION

The best meditation for joy is mindfulness throughout your day. Start your day by repeating the mantra to affirm your joy. Then, as you go through the day, try to remain focused in the moment. Whenever you find your mind wandering to the past or future, return your focus to the moment. Pay attention to all of the sensations that come throughout the day, whether it's the pleasurable feel of sunlight on your shoulders or the sound of beautiful music. Repeat the mantra whenever you find yourself wandering from your focus on the present time.

REMEDY #1: AMBER

Amber is one of the happiest stones I know. Whenever I really wish to cultivate joy, I wear a necklace or bracelet of amber, which instantly lifts my mood and helps me radiate joy. The next time you want to feel joyful, try wearing an amber necklace.

REMEDY #2: CITRINE

Citrine is another sunny, happy stone that helps you feel joyful. I like to carry citrine in my pocket every day. Whenever I start to lose present focus, I reach into my pocket and rub the citrine as a reminder to focus on the now.

 TIP: Experiencing more joy in your life doesn't mean ignoring negative emotions. All of your emotions are necessary and important, so you need to allow yourself to feel them. However, remaining focused on the present moment can allow you to experience joy, even in the midst of negative emotions.

Kindness

Kindness, love, and compassion go hand in hand, and all three arise from your heart chakra, which is where unconditional love forms. Treating people with kindness—no matter who they are or how they treat you—is a very powerful statement to the universe of your unconditional love for yourself and others. It is also an important reminder that you are one with everyone and everything around you. By treating others with kindness, you are treating yourself with kindness, as well.

I treat every living creature, including myself, with loving compassion and kindness.

MEDITATION

Whenever you encounter another person, take a moment to repeat the mantra a few times and visualize that person surrounded in a pure white light.

REMEDY #1: GREEN AVENTURINE HEART CHAKRA WORK

This heart chakra crystal sparks compassion and kindness—for yourself and others. Each day before you leave your house to encounter others, take a few moments to hold green aventurine to your heart chakra while repeating the mantra to yourself several times.

REMEDY #2: ROSE QUARTZ

Rose quartz is the universal stone of love. Keep a piece in your pocket. When you feel a less than kind action arising (and we all experience such things), reach into your pocket and touch the rose quartz, repeating the mantra to yourself three times or until the urge passes.

 TIP: Kindness is a conscious act that becomes easier the more you practice it. Try practicing simple acts of kindness throughout your day to strengthen your "kindness muscle." For example, resolve to offer a genuine smile to three strangers you typically wouldn't acknowledge, or pay a few people sincere compliments. By making it your mission to intentionally behave kindly to others, you will soon develop kindness as your second nature.

Laziness

Sometimes what we perceive as laziness—in ourselves or in others—isn't laziness at all, but rather a reaction to deep-seated fears or emotions. Other times, it arises from lack of initiative, as a reaction to feeling we have to do things we don't want to, exhaustion, or even just lack of inspiration. Whatever its root cause, healing laziness comes from finding the motivation and initiative to be an active participant in life instead of a passive one.

I am energized to take action to make things happen in my life.

MEDITATION

Sit or lie comfortably, repeating the mantra to yourself. Visualize yourself taking action on things that you have resisted, allowing the visualization to carry through to the results of having taken action. Visualize the specific outcomes you would like to see, noting your feelings of accomplishment and joy. Continue your meditation for at least 10 minutes.

REMEDY #1: CALCITE

Calcite is a stone that amplifies energy, so it can help you overcome inaction or laziness. While you can use any color calcite, orange calcite is a particularly good stone for spurring you to action. Upon awakening in the morning, sit with a piece of calcite in your receiving (nondominant) hand, repeating the mantra for 10 minutes or until you feel energized.

REMEDY #2: RAINBOW FLUORITE GRID

If laziness or procrastination at work is an issue, try making a simple triangular grid from rainbow fluorite, which can help focus your energy and spur you to action. Place one piece of fluorite as the center of the pyramid, and then place three pieces of fluorite around it to form the three points of the triangle. Have one point of the triangle pointing directly at you to direct energy toward you and amplify the energy moving away from you.

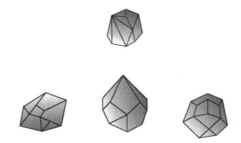

Letting Go

Letting go is an important part of accepting change and moving ahead with your life. It isn't always easy, however, because holding on to what is familiar is comfortable. Still, in many cases, the things you fail to let go of will hold you back, keeping you trapped in energetic patterns that no longer serve you and stopping you from moving forward on your spirit's path.

I release everything that no longer serves me.

MEDITATION

Sit or lie quietly and comfortably. Visualize all the patterns, emotions, ideas, and things you hold on to that no longer serve you. As you repeat the mantra, imagine those things lifting away from you and dissolving. Continue your meditation for at least 10 minutes.

REMEDY #1: LABRADORITE

This wonderful stone can help bring about release by allowing you to make transformative changes while stepping away from old patterns. It is an excellent stone for releasing deeply held beliefs, emotions, or patterns that no longer serve you. Sit quietly with your eyes closed and hold a piece of labradorite in your receiving (nondominant) hand. Ask, "What am I holding on to that is preventing me from moving forward on my path?" Note anything that arises. Now, transfer the labradorite to your giving (dominant) hand and state the mantra. Continue until you feel a sense of release or a lifting of the energy. Always cleanse and charge your labradorite after you perform this exercise.

REMEDY #2: ROSE QUARTZ & GREEN AVENTURINE HEART CHAKRA WORK

If you are holding on to emotional pain, try this combination of heart chakra stones. Hold one in each hand and focus on your heart chakra, repeating "let go" to yourself. Continue for 10 minutes or until you feel a sense of release and peace.

REMEDY #3: RHODOCHROSITE

If the letting go you need to do involves forgiving someone and releasing them from your anger or hurt, try using rhodochrosite. Sit with the rhodochrosite in your giving (dominant) hand and visualize the person you need to release. When you see that person in your mind's eye, repeat, "I forgive you. I release you," until you feel a lifting of your spirit. (Also see Forgiveness on page 120.)

Loneliness

Feelings of loneliness and isolation can occur even when you are surrounded by others. You may feel lonely because you lack companionship, or you may feel isolated because you choose to live your life in a way that others may not support or understand. Using crystals can help you overcome loneliness, or they can provide you with the courage you need to seek companionship.

I send love out into the universe, and in doing so, I attract love and friendship to me.

MEDITATION

Sit quietly with your eyes closed, breathing normally. Speak the mantra 10 times. Imagine your body as a glowing magnet of white light. For about 10 minutes, picture your white magnetizing light drawing others to you. Finish by repeating the mantra again 10 times.

REMEDY #1: CLEAR QUARTZ & ROSE QUARTZ GRID

In a place where you spend a majority of your time, set up the clear and rose quartz infinity grid described on page 30. The rose quartz will attract love and friendship, while the clear quartz will amplify and direct it.

REMEDY #2: RUTILATED QUARTZ

Rutilated quartz can help dispel loneliness. Carry a small piece in your pocket to attract companionship and ease feelings of loneliness.

 TIP: If you feel you lack love, friendship, and companionship in your life, this may be because you feel, on some level, that you are unlovable. Your solar plexus chakra is the source of self-esteem, so meditating while focusing on this chakra can help you feel worthy of companionship. Try meditating for at least 10 minutes using the mantra while holding yellow tigers eye to your solar plexus chakra to help overcome feelings associated with lack of self-worth.

Love

Whether you are seeking romantic love, spiritual love, or the love of friendship and companionship, you must first love yourself before you can love or accept love from others. Your heart chakra is the center of all of these forms of love, helping you achieve unconditional love for everything in the universe. Heart chakra stones can help increase your openness to giving and receiving love.

I radiate love to all, and love comes back to me a thousandfold.

MEDITATION

Sit quietly with your eyes closed and focus on your heart chakra. Imagine a green light coming from your heart chakra and going in all directions, filling the universe with your love. Visualize the green light of love coming back to you from all directions of the universe, filling you with love, as well. As you do this, repeat the mantra at least 10 times.

REMEDY #1: ROSE QUARTZ

Keep rose quartz with you at all times to help you stay rooted in unconditional love. Carry it as close to your heart chakra as possible. I keep it tucked into my bra, carry it in a shirt pocket, or wear it as a pendant on a long chain that falls to my heart chakra.

REMEDY #2: GARNET

Garnet inspires romantic love and passion. Keep garnet with you when you are seeking romantic love or hold it in your receiving (nondominant) hand as you meditate on finding a romantic partner.

REMEDY #3: CITRINE CHAKRA WORK

Citrine can help you obtain self-love by raising your self-esteem. This is a solar plexus chakra stone, but without self-esteem, self-love in the heart chakra isn't possible. Meditate with the citrine in your receiving (nondominant) hand pressed to your solar plexus chakra, with your giving (dominant) hand pressed to your heart chakra. Repeat the mantra, "I love myself, and I am worthy of love" at least 10 times. Feel the energy move from your solar plexus chakra up into your heart.

Luck

You've probably heard the saying, "You make your own luck," and it's true. The Law of Attraction says that the luck we have in our life comes from our attention to our thoughts, words, and actions, which make us magnets for luck, both good and bad. In other words, what you put out into the universe, you receive back. Thoughts, words, and actions all have energy that draws similar energy to you.

I send positive vibrations into the universe through my thoughts, words, and actions, and they return to me as good luck.

MEDITATION

Instead of meditating on being lucky, it's important to experience active living meditation, in which you consistently monitor the messages you send to the universe in thought, word, and deed. As you go through your day, pay attention to the thoughts you think, the words you speak, and the actions you take. If you catch yourself thinking, speaking, or acting in a manner contrary to the positive things you'd like to attract, immediately correct it. For example, if you catch yourself saying to a friend, "I have the worst luck!" say in your mind, "Cancel that. I consistently have good luck."

REMEDY #1: JADE

Jade is a gemstone of luck, so wearing jade jewelry is a great way to inspire luck to enter your life. Wear jade jewelry whenever you feel you need a little extra dose of luck.

REMEDY #2: CITRINE

This is a good luck stone that also summons financial abundance. So if it's luck in business you need, keep a piece of citrine on your desk, remembering to cleanse and charge it regularly to keep it working at its best.

REMEDY #3: ROSE QUARTZ

If you're looking to find luck in your love life, keep a piece of rose quartz near your heart chakra to help strengthen your romantic luck.

Meditation

The stones you choose to enhance your meditation will vary, depending on what you are trying to achieve. I've listed some stones in this section that help focus and clarify meditation. It's important to note, however, that virtually any crystal will help enhance meditation. For example, if you're working on a root chakra meditation, then root chakra stones like garnet will help, and so on.

I am one with the universe, and I connect to higher consciousness now.

MEDITATION

Sit or lie comfortably with your eyes closed, holding in either hand any of the recommended crystals that follow. Breathe normally, noticing your breathing without controlling it. Focus your attention in the area of your third eye, and notice any thoughts that arise without attaching to any of them. When thoughts arise, just allow them to drift away. Meditate for 15 to 30 minutes or longer.

REMEDY #1: SELENITE

Selenite is a stone of higher consciousness that can help you connect to a higher power while gaining clarity and focus. Hold the selenite in either hand.

REMEDY #2: SUPER SEVEN

This high-vibration stone has seven different crystals in it, so it is an excellent meditation stone. Hold or wear the stone while you meditate.

REMEDY #3: CLEAR QUARTZ

Clear quartz is a master healer, cleanser, and amplifier. You can use any shape or size of quartz, realizing that the larger the crystal, the more powerful it will be. Hold or wear the quartz when you meditate.

 TIP: Some people have a difficult sitting and performing mindfulness meditation. If you experience difficulty with this type of meditation, consider a more active meditation such as walking meditation, guided meditation, or visualization. All can help connect you to a higher Source.

Mood Swings

It's not always easy to stay on an emotionally even keel, nor is it always necessary. Throughout your life, you'll experience an incredible range of emotions, which is part of the human experience. These emotions are normal and healthy, provided you don't get trapped in any single negative emotion. Mood swings, however, often accompany hormonal issues, stress, and other difficulties, and they can be problematic in relationships. These remedies can help normalize erratic mood swings that may affect how you relate to others.

I manage my feelings with kindness and compassion for myself and others.

MEDITATION

The best meditation for mood swings is just simple deep breathing and mindfulness. When you feel your moods are unstable, close your eyes and take several deep breaths. As you breathe, repeat the mantra to yourself until you start to feel more even-keeled.

REMEDY #1: SMOKY QUARTZ

Smoky quartz is an excellent crystal for balancing emotions, so it's great to keep with you if you are suffering from mood swings related to reproductive system hormonal changes (such as PMS or menopause). During those times, carry a piece of smoky quartz with you in your pocket, near your sacral chakra, which controls these hormones. If you feel a mood swing kicking in, repeat the mantra 10 times.

REMEDY #2: SODALITE

You may also experience mood swings associated with other hormones, particularly from the thyroid and parathyroid. To help with these, focus on the throat chakra, wearing a piece of sodalite around your neck.

 TIP: Mood swings and irritability may also be related to nonhormonal personal issues such as stress, depression, or unexpressed anger. If your mood swings are related to these issues, follow the remedies in this chapter for dealing with them.

Motivation

It's not always easy to stay motivated, no matter what the task. Whether you're trying to make healthy changes to diet and exercise, remain focused and productive at work, or work toward any goal, it's easy to lose sight of the end result and lose motivation before you get there.

I am energized, focused on my goal [name the goal], and motivated to succeed.

MEDITATION

The mantra is more powerful when you combine it with visualization. Perform this visualization once or twice a day until you reach your goal. Sit or lie comfortably with your eyes closed, breathing normally. Imagine yourself already having achieved your goal, adding as much detail as you can. Visualize how you will feel, how you will look, and how your life will change as a result of achieving your goal. Repeat the mantra 10 times.

REMEDY #1: CARNELIAN

Carnelian spurs you to action. Whenever you need a boost of motivation, no matter what your task, carry a piece of carnelian with you. When you feel your motivation flagging, hold the carnelian, close your eyes, and repeat the mantra three or four times.

REMEDY #2: CLEAR QUARTZ & CARNELIAN GRID

If your motivation always seems to flag in one particular area of your home or office, make a grid and place it there. For example, if your snack cupboard starts calling to you at midnight and you're trying to lose a few pounds, place the grid on a low shelf in the cupboard. To make this grid, place a large carnelian in the middle for motivation. Then, place four clear quartz points in a square facing away from the center stone to amplify and direct the motivational energy outward.

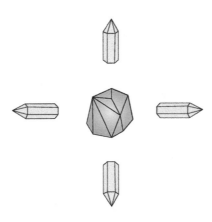

Negativity

It's easy to get trapped in a negative mind-set, especially when it feels as if things just aren't going well in your life. Unfortunately, getting stuck in a pattern of negativity creates an energy pattern that begets more negative energy, pulling you into a downward spiral. Use these remedies to turn the pattern around.

I release negativity and enter into a positive new future.

MEDITATION

Close your eyes and visualize negativity as a dark cloud lifting out of your body and into the atmosphere. Then, once the negative energy has dissipated, visualize white light entering your body and surrounding you.

REMEDY #1: SMOKY QUARTZ

Smoky quartz is one of the best crystals available for turning negativity around into positive energy. If you're stuck in a negative pattern, work with smoky quartz as often as possible, sleeping with it under your pillow, carrying it in your pocket, and placing it in strategic locations around your home or office.

REMEDY #2: BLACK TOURMALINE

Use black tourmaline to block negativity from another person. If you are going to be around a negative person, carry the tourmaline with you and, if possible, place it in a position between you and the other person, such as in your front pocket if you are facing the person.

 TIP: If a negative coworker is affecting you, tape black tourmaline to the bottom of your desk chair, or keep it somewhere between your desk and your coworker's desk. You can even tape black tourmaline to the bottom of your coworker's chair to absorb the negative energy before it has a chance to travel to you.

Obsession/Compulsion

Obsessions and compulsions are two sides of the same coin. Obsessive thoughts often arise from anxiety, while compulsion is a repetitive behavior that helps relieve some of that anxiety. These remedies can help you relieve the anxiety without resorting to compulsions, and they can be used as a complement to professional behavioral therapy.

I embrace the uncertainty of life and choose to live peacefully within it.

MEDITATION

One of the issues that arises with obsession and compulsion is that your mind gets stuck in a thought loop. When this occurs, close your eyes and breathe deeply, repeating the mantra several times until you have reset your thoughts.

REMEDY #1: AMETRINE

Ametrine is a combination of amethyst and citrine, both of which can calm any compulsions and obsessions while helping to relax your mind. Amethyst is a third eye chakra stone, which controls your thoughts, while citrine is a solar plexus chakra stone, which affects your self-image. Carry ametrine with you, and when you notice obsessive thoughts and compulsive behavior starting, hold it in your hand as you repeat the mantra 10 times.

REMEDY #2: HERKIMER DIAMOND

Wear a Herkimer diamond around your neck to help release and relieve stress and calm you. This can support you as you learn new thought processes, amplifying the work you are doing with your therapist to relieve your obsessive thoughts and compulsive behaviors.

REMEDY #3: CITRINE & AMETHYST CHAKRA WORK

Lie on your back with a piece of amethyst on your third eye chakra and a piece of citrine on your solar plexus chakra. Visualize energy flowing between the two chakras. Do this daily for at least 10 minutes, cleansing your crystals after use, until you feel the hold your obsession has on you is lessening.

Opening the Heart

Our hearts can close for a number of reasons. When they do, we limit our own potential for joy. A closed heart blocks the flow of energy through your heart chakra, which sits in the very center of the chakras. This prevents the free flow of energy between your chakras, which can throw you entirely out of balance. Therefore, it's extremely important to keep this chakra open, both for yourself and for all your relationships.

My heart is open to giving and receiving love.

MEDITATION

Lie on your back comfortably, breathing normally. Place both hands gently over your heart chakra. Imagine your heart chakra as a swirling ball of green energy. Bring white light in through your crown chakra and watch as it flows through each of the chakras, down through the heart chakra, eventually exiting through your root chakra. Repeat the mantra at the beginning and end of the meditation.

REMEDY #1: ROSE QUARTZ HEART

You can find stones carved into an array of shapes, including hearts. While it may seem a bit literal, the symbolism of a rose quartz heart works here for opening your heart. Hold a rose quartz heart during the meditation, allowing its unconditional loving energy to fill your heart chakra.

REMEDY #2: RUBY

Ruby is another crystal that activates your heart chakra. Wear a ruby pendant around your neck to open this chakra. Be sure to cleanse and charge the ruby daily.

 TIP: While the first remedy calls for a rose quartz heart, it isn't necessary. You can use any piece of rose quartz in any shape that you find appealing. To find the right one for you, hold it in your receiving (nondominant) hand with your giving (dominant) hand over your heart and your eyes closed. Choose the piece of rose quartz that sends a warm feeling of love from your receiving hand into your heart.

Overindulgence

Overindulgence is something we all do from time to time. Occasional bouts of excess usually don't do much harm, but when they become habitual, they can throw your body, mind, and spirit out of balance. While many people think of overindulgence in terms of food and drink, you can overindulge in many things, such as spending money or watching television. In its most out-of-control state, overindulgence can lead to addiction. Please see Addiction on page 58 for help.

I choose to satisfy my mind, body, and spirit with things that support my highest good.

MEDITATION

If you find yourself in a pattern of overindulgence, paying attention to what is driving the urge to overindulge can help prevent it. When you catch yourself starting to overindulge or having the urge to do so, close your eyes and focus your breathing. Ask yourself, "What feeling am I having that is driving this behavior?" Pay attention to the answer that arises, and then imagine that feeling lifting away from your body and dissolving. Finish by repeating the mantra three times.

REMEDY #1: AMETHYST

Since overindulgence is closely related to addiction, try using the sobriety stone, amethyst. If you catch yourself in a pattern of over-indulgence, carry amethyst in your pocket and hold it in your receiving (nondominant) hand as you try to resist temptation. Be sure to cleanse and recharge the amethyst daily if you find yourself using it frequently.

REMEDY #2: GARNET

Garnet can help foster balance and prevent overindulgence. Place a piece of garnet under your mattress or pillow at night to help change your mind-set while you sleep.

 TIP: If you tend to overindulge in a certain area of your home or office—such as eating an entire bag of potato chips while watching television—tape a piece of amethyst or garnet to your usual chair or couch in that room.

Passion

Passion is about more than love and sex, although it certainly is an important factor in those feelings. Passion is about living life with gusto and finding intense interest in and enjoyment of the activities you choose. Living life with passion puts you on a path toward joy and fulfillment, and following your passions can help keep you on your spirit's path. Igniting passion in all aspects of your life can help you live your life more vibrantly and fully.

I embrace everything in my life with passion and joy.

MEDITATION

Sit quietly with your eyes closed, breathing deeply. Visualize your heart chakra opening and a vibrant white light shining from it. Become the white light, repeating the mantra. Do this for 10 minutes.

REMEDY #1: PINK TOURMALINE

Pink tourmaline is a stone that ignites romantic passion. Keep pink tourmaline on the bedside tables on both sides of your bed to help ignite passion in your relationship.

REMEDY #2: PYRITE

This golden stone awakens vitality, enabling you to live your life with more passion and creativity. To increase your passion for your work, tape a piece of pyrite to the bottom of your work chair, or keep a piece on your desk.

REMEDY #3: GARNET ROOT CHAKRA WORK

To inspire passion in your relationship and increase your sex drive, look to the red root chakra crystals. In this case, use garnet. Lie on your back and place a garnet on your root chakra. Visualize your chakra as a red swirling light. Feel the garnet adding its energy to your chakra. Be sure to cleanse the stone when you are done.

Peace

Peace is an internal process that allows you to feel calm and tranquil, even during times of turmoil. Peace exists within you, so finding ways to cultivate this characteristic can carry you through difficult times with grace. Peace is not, however, a lack of emotion. Rather, it is a calm place that helps you act from love instead of reacting from fear.

I am at peace with all aspects of my life.

MEDITATION

Sit or lie quietly in a comfortable position with your eyes closed. Breathe deeply and recite the mantra, feeling peace fill you as you inhale and tension leave you as you exhale. Do this for at least 10 minutes or until you feel deep peace.

REMEDY #1: BLUE AVENTURINE

Blue aventurine facilitates a deep sense of inner peace. Hold this stone during the meditation. You can also use blue aventurine throughout the day if you need an infusion of peace. Hold it in your receiving (nondominant) hand and take several deep breaths, allowing calm to descend upon you.

REMEDY #2: BLUE LACE AGATE

If you're ever feeling jumpy and out of sorts, blue lace agate can help you overcome this, returning you to a state of peaceful alertness. Keep a piece in your desk drawer or pocket, and hold it in your receiving (nondominant) hand as you breathe deeply whenever you start to feel stressed.

 TIP: Visualization is very effective at restoring peace, and it takes only a moment or two. Visualize a happy, quiet, peaceful place and imagine yourself sitting in that spot for just a moment or two, allowing the peace to wash over you. You can do this holding either of the crystals mentioned to enhance the effects of the visualization.

Phobias

Phobias are extreme, unreasonable fears that are usually anxiety-related. Typically, a person with a phobia knows logically that he or she doesn't need to fear that object, but still fears it. For example, I have a snake phobia, and even though I know the snakes where I live are harmless, I almost always respond unreasonably when I see them. Crystals can be helpful for relieving the anxiety associated with phobias.

I am calm and fearless when faced with [name the phobia]. I am safe, well, and relaxed.

MEDITATION

Since the goal of meditation is peace, visualizing what you are afraid of may not work here, because even the visualization may cause stress and anxiety. Instead, use a meditation when you are truly faced with that fear (such as if you fear flying but have to get on a plane). Close your eyes and breathe deeply. Repeat the mantra 10 times, seeing yourself as calm, safe, and relaxed after having faced your fear.

REMEDY #1: RUTILATED QUARTZ

Many phobias arise from deeper issues, such as past trauma or deeply held beliefs and emotions. Uncovering the root of this phobia is one of the first steps in helping to clear it. Holding a piece of rutilated quartz in your hand, close your eyes and breathe deeply. Ask, "What is the cause of my [name] phobia?" Now, see what arises. Once you understand the root, visualize it leaving your body and dissolving into the atmosphere.

REMEDY #2: AZURITE

Azurite may help relieve phobias in some people. If you know you will be faced with your phobias, carry it with you in your pocket. For example, I carry azurite whenever I work in the garden, mow the grass, or go hiking.

Positive Energy

Increasing positive energy can help make your life more vibrant and joyful. While it would be wonderful to bounce through life always brimming with positive energy, the truth is, from time to time, things happen that take away some of that positivity. When this occurs, you can take steps to attract positive energy back into your life.

I look forward to positive things manifesting in my life today and every day.

MEDITATION

Sit quietly with your eyes closed, breathing normally. Visualize any negative energy you have accumulated leaving your body. Now, repeating the mantra, visualize vibrant white light coming from above and entering through your crown chakra, moving down through all of your chakras, and filling your body. Allow the white light to lift your energy. Do this for at least 10 minutes.

REMEDY #1: CLEAR QUARTZ

To increase positive energy, you need to cleanse your aura and remove negative energy. Clear quartz is a master cleansing stone, which will help recharge your aura with positive energy and remove negative energy. To use it, hold the quartz in your receiving (nondominant) hand as you sit comfortably with your eyes closed, breathing normally. Visualize the energy from the stone flowing into your receiving hand and then into your body, filling your body with positive energy. Watch as the energy projects out from your body and into your aura, filling it with positive energy.

REMEDY #2: SMOKY QUARTZ

Smoky quartz has a very positive vibration, and it can turn negative energy into positive energy. I like to carry a smoky quartz crystal in my pocket to keep and increase my positive energy. Cleanse the quartz crystal and recharge it daily, since it is not only increasing positive vibrations, but also absorbing negative energy.

Prosperity

Being truly prosperous in life is about more than having plenty of money. True prosperity dwells in body, mind, and spirit, bringing you health, happiness, good relationships, fulfilling work, plenty of love, and financial well-being. Many people struggle with prosperity because they believe they don't deserve it, or that in being prosperous, they will be taking it away from someone else. Both of these beliefs are fallacies.

I am prosperous in all aspects of my life, and I am grateful for that prosperity.

MEDITATION

Sit comfortably with your eyes closed, breathing normally. As you repeat the mantra, imagine that your entire body is a large magnet, drawing health, wealth, joy, and love to you. Continue for at least 10 minutes.

REMEDY #1: CITRINE

Citrine is one of the most effective money stones. Place a piece of citrine where you keep your cash, such as in your wallet, money drawer, or cash register. Don't forget to cleanse and recharge the citrine at least once a week to keep it active.

REMEDY #2: AVENTURINE

Green aventurine is a heart stone that can create balance, enabling you to experience prosperity in all aspects of your life, rather than focusing on only one type of prosperity, such as abundance. The balancing energy of this stone enables you to keep your consciousness focused on all forms of prosperity, so carry it with you as you go about your day.

TIP: Many people harm their ability to be prosperous with their thoughts and beliefs. They may catch themselves thinking, "Gosh, I'm so broke," "I can't afford that," or "My health is so poor." These are limiting thoughts that work with the Law of Attraction, so it's important not to put that energy out there. If you catch yourself thinking these types of thoughts, immediately say in your mind, "Cancel that. I am grateful I have [fill in the blank]." This negates the anti-prosperity thinking, reinforces a prosperity mind-set, and expresses gratitude to the universe for providing.

SPIRITUAL
Protection

As you go through life, you sometimes come into contact with people or circumstances that may affect you negatively. This can harm your spirit by causing a loss of positive energy, an increase of negative energy, or similar effects. Damaging influences can come from negative situations, people with bad intentions, or other adverse circumstance. Some crystals can offer spiritual protection by absorbing the negativity.

I surround myself with a protective white light of spiritual energy.

MEDITATION

Visualize a white light surrounding you as you repeat the mantra for at least 10 minutes. Push the white light from your core, allowing it to extend around you. The white light can take on any form that feels safe. For example, I push a bubble of white light from my core until it surrounds me completely (or, in some cases, surrounds my home and family, as well). Push the light out from your core as opposed to building it around you, so that you don't trap any outside negativity in your shield of light.

REMEDY #1: BLACK TOURMALINE

Black tourmaline is my go-to stone of spiritual protection. I carry it with me all the time in my pocket. You can also wear it around your neck as a pendant or use some other piece of jewelry that contains black tourmaline. Because it is blocking negative energy all the time and providing protection, it needs to be cleansed and recharged daily.

REMEDY #2: AMETHYST

Protect against negative energy and purify your energy at the same time with a piece of amethyst crystal. This is a great crystal to protect your spirit from negative energies associated with nightmares or those that arise while you sleep. Place the amethyst under your pillow before you go to sleep at night. Cleanse and recharge the crystal each night before you go to bed.

TIP: When you first start using the shield described in the meditation, it may not stay in place very long. Therefore, it's best to apply it several times throughout the day. Eventually, you'll get better at keeping it in place during the day. You can also use this shield and put it in place whenever you feel you are entering a negative situation.

Relationships

Having healthy relationships involves a number of factors, including self-esteem, love, and communication, which are all qualities of the three middle chakras: the solar plexus, the heart, and the throat. Using crystals that concentrate on these chakras can help strengthen your relationships.

I have healthy, productive, and happy relationships.

MEDITATION

Perform this meditation with the person with whom you are in a relationship, romantic or otherwise. Sit comfortably facing each other. Place one hand in the center of your partner's chest and have your partner place one hand in the center of your chest, over the heart chakra. Synchronize your breathing so that as one of you exhales, the other inhales. As your partner exhales, visualize energy coming from him or her and entering as you inhale. As you exhale, visualize your energy entering your partner. Visualize that energy traveling from your nose down through your throat chakra, heart chakra, and solar plexus chakra. As you each do this, repeat the mantra silently to yourselves. Sit this way for at least 10 minutes.

REMEDY #1: LAPIS LAZULI

To improve how you communicate with a loved one, lie on your back with a piece of lapis lazuli on your heart chakra for 10 minutes. When you need an extra communication boost with that person, wear a lapis lazuli pendant around your neck to facilitate the conversation.

REMEDY #2: ROSE QUARTZ

One of the greatest gifts we can give and receive in relationships is unconditional love. Rose quartz facilitates unconditional love. Carry a piece with you whenever you spend time with your loved ones.

REMEDY #3: YELLOW TIGERS EYE

To truly love another, you must love and accept yourself. Therefore, working on the solar plexus chakra issue of self-love is essential in relationships. Hold a piece of yellow tigers eye in your hand, close your eyes, and repeat to yourself, "I love and accept myself unconditionally." Do this three times.

Repression

Sometimes when we fear our emotions or they feel too overwhelming, we repress them. While repression may serve as a temporary coping mechanism, when you repress your emotions habitually, you risk blocking emotional release altogether. Emotional release is necessary for mental, emotional, and spiritual health.

I allow myself to fully experience my emotions, and they pass through me quickly.

MEDITATION

Sit quietly with your eyes closed, breathing normally. Speak the mantra. Pay attention to any spots of tension in your body where you may feel an unreleased emotion. Place your hands gently on that spot and repeat the mantra for at least 10 minutes. Allow the emotion to release from the spot and wash over you, allowing yourself to feel it fully before releasing it.

REMEDY #1: BOJI STONES

Boji Stones offer a powerful way to release emotional repression. Hold the stones while you do the meditation.

REMEDY #2: RHODOCHROSITE

Once you've released the repressed emotions, it is time to facilitate emotional healing. Use rhodochrosite to do this. Carry the crystal in your pocket every day for a week after you've released the repressed emotions, or longer if you feel you need it. Cleanse and recharge the stone daily.

Resentment

When you refuse to acknowledge or express your anger, it can become resentment. Resentment often arises out of unmet expectations, and it is damaging to you, as well as to others. It can harm relationships, making obstacles seem insurmountable. The thing about resentment is that while you may feel that someone else has treated you unfairly, the other person may not feel the treatment was unfair, or may not even know he or she did anything you found upsetting. Finding ways to deal with your resentment can help heal your relationship.

I release all anger and resentment and replace those feelings with unconditional love.

MEDITATION

Close your eyes and sit comfortably, breathing normally. Focus on your resentment, noting where you feel it in your body. Now, push loving energy from your heart chakra to wherever it is, allowing the warm heart energy to dissolve the resentment. As you do so, repeat the mantra. Do this for at least 10 minutes or until your resentment fades.

REMEDY #1: ROSE QUARTZ

Rose quartz, a stone of unconditional love, can help you expel resent-ment. Since resentment arises so often from unmet expectations, when you view another with unconditional love, you release any expectation and focus only on the love you have for that person. When you're feeling resentment, lie with a piece of rose quartz on your heart chakra as you focus on sending unconditional love to the other person.

REMEDY #2: PERIDOT

This beautiful green stone is a heart chakra stone that can help release any negative emotions you have toward another, including anger, resentment, or jealousy. Hold this stone gently over your heart chakra as you do the meditation.

 TIP: You can't release your resentment until you acknowledge it. If you are experiencing negative feelings toward another person but don't know why, ask yourself why as you drift off to sleep that night. In the morning, record any dreams or insights you had to help you identify the source of your resentment.

Self-Control

Sometimes it feels good to let yourself get a little out of control. Occasionally, we all give in and indulge, and this can be good for the spirit. However, if you habitually lack self-control and it is keeping you from walking your true path or attaining your goals, then it may be time to reassess and take action.

I am fully in control of my actions.

MEDITATION

Mindfulness meditation is a way of exerting self-control, because it teaches you to focus and not allow your thoughts to run away from you. In this case, focus on the mantra, repeating it over and over. If other thoughts arise during the mantra, notice them and gently release them without getting caught up in any specific thought. Use the mantra to focus you and help you maintain control throughout the meditation, which should last for at least 10 minutes.

REMEDY #1: ONYX

Self-control originates in the root chakra, which is why this powerful root chakra stone works so well to help you develop self-mastery. Onyx grounds you and helps you maintain determination as you progress toward your goal. Use an onyx stone when you perform grounding and centering (see page 128 and 66). Cleanse and charge this stone daily after use.

REMEDY #2: RED JASPER

Red jasper, another root chakra stone, can help you maintain self-discipline, which keeps you in control. Carry red jasper with you in your pants pocket, touching or holding it throughout the day when you feel your self-control slipping.

 TIP: Try meditating with onyx or red jasper on your root chakra at the start of your day to help you maintain self-control throughout the day. Lie on your back with the stone on your root chakra. Visualize the chakra swirling red, receiving energy from the stone.

Self-Esteem/ Self-Worth

Many things can happen throughout our lives that affect our self-worth. We may internalize messages we hear in our childhood and carry them with us throughout our lives, we may behave in ways that aren't consistent with our integrity, or we may have failed relationships that make us feel unworthy of love. Self-esteem is a solar plexus chakra issue, and without it, it is difficult to find joy and peace in our lives.

I love myself, and I am worthy of love and respect.

MEDITATION

Because self-esteem is so closely tied to the solar plexus chakra, a meditation focusing on opening this chakra can help you build your self-esteem. Lie on your back with your hands placed gently on your solar plexus chakra. Breathe normally. Visualize golden light coming from the universe, into your hands, and into your chakra. Picture the chakra as a growing, swirling golden-yellow light and allow its energy to flow throughout your body. As you do this, repeat the mantra. Do this for at least 10 minutes, ideally for several days in a row.

REMEDY #1: CITRINE

This golden stone is the embodiment of the color of the solar plexus chakra. It is a powerful stone that helps promote feelings of self-esteem and self-worth, so it's an excellent crystal if you are struggling with self-esteem. To use citrine for self-esteem, set it on your solar plexus chakra as you do the meditation. You can also carry it with you and hold it whenever you feel your self-esteem start to flag. As you hold the citrine in your receiving (nondominant) hand, repeat the mantra, 10 times.

REMEDY #2: HEMATITE

Hematite is a root chakra stone, but it is also a strong builder of self-worth. You can find very inexpensive hematite rings online or in crystal shops. Wear one, cleansing it every few days.

Self-Harm/ Self-Sabotage

Many people sabotage themselves without even realizing they are doing so. Others do it deliberately. Either way, self-harm and self-sabotage can manifest in a multitude of ways, such as in thrill-seeking or dangerous behavior, drug or alcohol addictions, eating disorders, or cutting addiction. If you are self-harming, it is important that you seek professional help, because your life may depend on it.

I deserve to be well, so I exercise care in supporting my own well-being.

MEDITATION

Positive affirmation may be one of the most effective types of meditation for moving beyond a self-sabotaging mind-set. You can use the mantra, but I also recommend making a list of your own personal affirmations. These should be positive thoughts about yourself, such as, "I am happy and at peace," "I am successful in all my endeavors," and "I look forward to good things happening in my life, today and every day." Recite each of your affirmations three times daily in the mirror, meeting your own eyes as you do so.

REMEDY #1: BLACK TOURMALINE

Black tourmaline, a root chakra stone, works like a sponge, absorbing any negative thoughts or energy. It can work to block other's negative energy, and it can also absorb any of your own negativity. Wear black tourmaline around your neck as a pendant, making sure you cleanse and recharge it daily. You can also keep a piece of black tourmaline on your bedside table.

REMEDY #2: OBSIDIAN

Obsidian is another stone that can help remove negative thoughts. When you feel yourself spiraling into a negative thought pattern, hold the obsidian in your receiving (nondominant) hand, and repeat the mantra or your affirmations 10 times.

 TIP: Depression often sits at the root of urges toward self-harm or self-sabotage. Use the remedies, mantra, and meditation for depression found on page 98 in conjunction with these remedies.

Shadows

We all have shadows we hide deep within ourselves that we don't wish to acknowledge. We so fear these aspects of our personality that we worry if they are exposed to the light, others will be unable to love us and we will be unable to love ourselves. So we keep them hidden, hoping they never rear their heads. If you look in a shadowy corner, you may indeed see something dark, but as soon as you shine a light there, the shadow disappears. The same is true of our shadow selves. When we expose it to the light of consciousness, the shadow is no longer frightening, and we can reintegrate that aspect of our personality into our whole being.

I lovingly and respectfully acknowledge every aspect of myself.

MEDITATION

Lie on your back with your eyes closed, breathing normally. Visualize your shadow aspects as actual dark shadows in your body. As you repeat the mantra for at least 10 minutes, watch those shadows lift away from you and dissipate.

REMEDY #1: BLACK TOURMALINE

Use black tourmaline to draw out your shadows and send them down the drain. Fill a bath with warm water and add ¼ cup of Himalayan pink salt or sea salt and one or two pieces of black tourmaline. Bathe for at least 10 minutes, and then remove the tourmaline from the tub and allow the water to run down the drain. Remain in the tub and visualize the shadows going down the drain with the water. Get out of the tub when the water has completely drained. Cleanse the crystal before you use it again.

REMEDY #2: ROSE QUARTZ

When you love yourself unconditionally, that means the whole of you, including your shadows. Use rose quartz to help you develop self-love, even for your shadow parts. Hold rose quartz as you do the meditation.

Shame

Many people confuse guilt and shame. While the two often go hand in hand, guilt is about something you did, and shame is about who you are. Guilt is often constructive, enabling you to readjust your behavior, while shame tends to be destructive, burrowing into your psyche. Shame is a deep and painful emotion that can keep you from fully loving yourself and prevent you from walking the true path of your spirit. Dealing with and releasing shame is necessary if you are to live a life of joy.

I am a good person and I walk my path with self-love.

MEDITATION

Shame tends to be a very visceral emotion that you can feel in your body. Close your eyes and reflect on your shame, noticing where you feel it. Now, send loving light to that spot, using it to gently dissolve your shame as you repeat the mantra for at least 10 minutes.

REMEDY #1: AMETHYST

Amethyst is a soothing and healing crystal that can help you release feelings of shame. If you experience chronic shame, carry amethyst with you at all times, making sure to cleanse and charge it daily.

REMEDY #2: TURQUOISE

Wear turquoise jewelry to release shame. Turquoise is a gemstone that works very well for releasing deep-rooted shame.

Shyness/ Social Anxiety

Shyness and social anxiety manifest as discomfort around other people. I am an introvert, so I understand how it feels to be shy or anxious in some social situations. However, the nature of the work I do often requires me to interact with many other people, so I've had to work at overcoming my social anxiety. Know that it is possible to come out of your shell with some assistance, including crystal healing.

I am outgoing and confident when interacting with others and meeting new people.

MEDITATION

Sit or lie comfortably, breathing normally. Visualize yourself going about your day and meeting new people. In your visualization, see yourself interacting in a friendly and confident manner. Do this for at least 10 minutes while repeating the mantra.

REMEDY #1: YELLOW TIGERS EYE SOLAR PLEXUS CHAKRA WORK

Yellow tigers eye is a solar plexus chakra stone that can greatly boost your social confidence. Before social occasions, do the meditation with yellow tigers eye resting on your solar plexus chakra to boost your self-confidence and relieve shyness.

REMEDY #2: MALACHITE

This beautiful green stone has a soothing energy that can calm your anxiety in social situations and foster friendliness. Carry a piece of malachite in your pocket whenever you know you're going to be in a situation that may make you feel socially anxious.

REMEDY #3: CITRINE

Citrine is another solar plexus chakra stone that boosts self-confidence and can also help you feel friendlier in unfamiliar situations. Wear a citrine pendant or carry a stone whenever you will be in a large group.

Stress

We live in a stressful world, and many people experience chronic elevated stress levels as a result. Chronic stress causes a mild but persistent fight-or-flight response, which in turn causes your adrenal glands to release hormones such as cortisol into your body. Chronically elevated stress levels can affect all aspects of your life, including your physical, mental, emotional, and spiritual well-being.

I am at peace and poised, knowing that all is well.

MEDITATION

My favorite stress meditation is what I call my happy place meditation. For me, my happy place is a beautiful meadow of tall wildflowers with snowcapped mountains in the background. I'm sure you have a happy place as well. When you feel stressed, breathe deeply into your belly. Repeat the mantra and visualize yourself sitting in your happy place (feel free to borrow mine) until you feel more relaxed. I use my happy place meditation so often that I go there immediately to relieve stress in just a few deep breaths.

REMEDY #1: BLUE LACE AGATE

I get calm just looking at blue lace agate, with its soothing blue color and its intriguing bands of white. This soothing stone is perfect for when you feel stressed out. You can just hold the stone in your hand and stare deeply into its depths, or you can keep it in your pocket to ward off stress.

REMEDY #2: BLUE KYANITE

Blue kyanite is another of my favorite stress stones. I have a long, slender piece of blue kyanite that I use as a worry stone, rubbing my thumb along it until I feel calm. You can use a piece of blue kyanite for this purpose as well.

Trust

In today's world, it can be difficult to have trust in much of anything. However, trusting our relationships, spirituality, ourselves, and our emotions is important. Learning to trust may be more difficult if you grew up in a situation in which you didn't feel you could trust people. But now you can begin to build trust on all levels.

I trust in the universe to provide everything I need on my spirit's path.

MEDITATION

Sit quietly with your eyes closed, breathing normally. Focus on your root chakra, which is where safety and security develop. Imagine your root chakra glowing red, as a spinning ball of light. Now, imagine white light from the universe entering your chakra and mixing with the red light. As you do this, repeat the mantra for at least 10 minutes.

REMEDY #1: BLUE CHALCEDONY

If you have difficulty trusting yourself, use blue chalcedony, which clears away self-doubt and strengthens your sense of self-trust. Carry it in your pocket, making sure to cleanse and recharge it daily.

REMEDY #2: SODALITE

Sodalite is a stone that promotes truth and trust, so it is excellent stone if you are experiencing trust issues in your relationship. Carry sodalite with you whenever you are with the person with whom you are experiencing trust issues.

 TIP: Trust in the universe boils down to having faith. If you experience universal mistrust, use the remedies for faith on page 116.

Willpower

Willpower is a fickle thing. Sometimes you have it, and other times it seems it is nowhere to be found. Having the willpower to delay short-term gratification is necessary if you want to achieve the long-term goals you desire. Willpower plays a role in so many aspects of life—from taking steps toward a dream to avoiding habits you know negatively affect your health. Fortunately, there is support for those times when your willpower seems lacking.

I always exercise willpower when I need it because I am dedicated to long-term success.

MEDITATION

The purpose of willpower is to achieve your goals, whatever they may be. Therefore, visualizing yourself as already having achieved your goals can help you maintain the willpower to get from point A to point B. Sit quietly and comfortably, breathing normally. Visualize yourself in the aftermath of having attained your goal, experiencing the emotional, spiritual, mental, and physical sensations associated with that. Continue the visualization for at least 10 minutes.

REMEDY #1: CITRINE SOLAR PLEXUS CHAKRA WORK

Willpower is a solar plexus chakra issue, which is where you define yourself and your boundaries. Essentially, willpower is a boundary that you have set for yourself. Lie on your back with a piece of citrine on your solar plexus chakra for 10 minutes at the start of each day to boost your willpower.

REMEDY #2: ONYX ROOT CHAKRA WORK

Willpower can also originate in your root chakra, where you form your identity. Sit holding a piece of onyx in your receiving (nondominant) hand as you focus on your root chakra, imagining it as red spinning light. Maintain this focus for at least 10 minutes.

 TIP: If you have specific objects in your home that challenge your willpower, such as sweets for your kids when you're trying to lose weight, keep a piece of citrine stored near that object to boost your willpower whenever you are near it. Be sure to cleanse and recharge the stone about once a week to maintain its potency.

Worry

Some people are bigger worriers than others, but we all worry from time to time. Often, the things we worry about are far beyond our control, so all we are doing is wasting energy that could be spent elsewhere. Worrying also sparks negative thinking, which through the Law of Attraction, may attract the exact circumstances into your life about which you are worrying.

My mind is relaxed, focused, clear, and free.

MEDITATION

I find that worries often arise when I am trying to quiet my mind, so I've developed a technique for dealing with that. Sit quietly with your eyes closed, breathing normally. In your mind's eye, picture a chalkboard. Now, ask your worries to rise up. As they do, picture them written on the chalkboard and say, "Erase," visualizing an eraser wiping away each worry. Replace each worry that arises with a positive affirmation of the opposite, so if the worry comes up, "I can't afford to pay my rent this month," erase it and replace it with, "I have all the resources I need to pay all my bills." You can also use this technique if you tend to worry as you drift off to sleep at night.

REMEDY #1: LABRADORITE

Select a thin, flat piece of labradorite to use as a worry stone. Labradorite can help calm your mind when it goes into worry mode. When it does, hold the piece of labradorite and rub your thumb back and forth across its surface while repeating the mantra until you feel your mind relax.

REMEDY #2: BLUE LACE AGATE

This soothing stone can help dispel worry. I recommend selecting a smooth, flat piece that you can use as a worry stone whenever your mind goes into overdrive. Again, hold the stone and rub your thumb back and forth across the surface while repeating the mantra until you feel your mind relax.

REMEDY #3: AMETHYST

Are you a night worrier? If so, slip a calming amethyst crystal under your pillow before going to bed. It will quiet your mind and help you sleep. Repeat the mantra as you drift off.

Crystal Remedies for Overlapping Areas

Our greatest challenges and our deepest desires tend not to present themselves in isolation. As such, we can activate crystals to help us in an even more holistic way when we apply them to one or more emotions or aspirations that often affect us in combination. While some of the remedies in this chapter call for multiple crystals, a greater number require only a couple of crystals to counteract dark impulses and move you toward light and hope.

Addiction & Self-Control

Addiction is an emotional, mental, spiritual, and physical issue. While the drive and urge for your substance of choice is biological, the roots of addiction are often buried deep within your psyche, the result of emotional or spiritual wounds. Sobriety, then, requires a combination of physical, spiritual, and emotional support and self-control. These remedies will provide support for all aspects of your recovery.

All the choices I make support my mental, physical, emotional, and spiritual health.

MEDITATION

Sit comfortably with your eyes closed, breathing normally. While repeating the mantra, visualize yourself easily and comfortably exercising self-control over any temptations that arise, and picture making healthy choices that support your well-being. Continue your meditation for about 10 minutes. Throughout the day, if you are faced with temptations or urges, close your eyes and repeat the mantra a few times.

REMEDY #1: MULTI-STONE FULL CHAKRA SUPPORT

Addiction often affects all of your chakras, so it is important to support yourself fully. Provide yourself with emotional and physical support while strengthening your resolve and self-control by lying on your back for 10 minutes with the following stones on each chakra:

- Obsidian on your root chakra
- Carnelian on your sacral chakra
- Citrine on your solar plexus chakra
- Peridot on your heart chakra
- Iolite on your throat chakra
- Amethyst on your third eye chakra
- Clear quartz on your crown chakra

REMEDY #2: AMETHYST & CARNELIAN

These two stones support sobriety—amethyst is a direct sobriety stone and carnelian is a stone of motivation and self-control. Carry these two stones in your pocket and hold them in your receiving (nondominant) hand for strength as needed throughout the day.

Anger & Forgiveness

Anger toward another is often justified, but when you hold on to it for an extended time, it hurts you more than it hurts the object of your ire. Forgiveness is an important step in releasing yourself and moving forward so you don't get stuck in negativity. Anger and forgiveness are emotions of the solar plexus chakra, so working to unblock that chakra can help you learn to release your anger and forgive.

I release all anger toward [person's name] and release [him/her] into a positive new future.

MEDITATION

Lie on your back with a yellow tigers eye on your solar plexus chakra, with both hands gently placed over the stone. Focus your attention on your solar plexus. As you focus on your chakra, repeat the mantra for at least 10 minutes or until you feel release. You can use any of the solar plexus stones for this meditation.

REMEDY #1: PREHNITE & CLEAR QUARTZ

Sitting comfortably, hold a piece of clear quartz in one hand and a piece of prehnite in the other hand. Repeat the mantra for 10 minutes or until you feel peace.

REMEDY #2: SMOKY QUARTZ & ROSE QUARTZ GRID

Smoky quartz helps transform powerful negative emotions, while rose quartz encourages forgiveness and unconditional love for self and others. To make the grid, place rose quartz of any shape in the center. Then, surround it with a square of four smoky quartz pieces. Using your finger, trace the shape of the grid, visualizing the object of your anger in your mind and surrounding them in white light. This powerful grid can help ease feelings of anger, turning them into forgiveness and love.

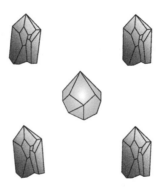

TIP: Sometimes the person with whom you are angry is yourself. For self-forgiveness, picture yourself as the object of your anger, and focus on releasing your anger toward yourself.

Denial & Acceptance

Denial can prevent you from acknowledging all sorts of issues in your life—from addictions to relationship problems to illnesses. Denial is a defense mechanism people sometimes use to avoid overwhelming emotions, but it also keeps you from moving forward in your life in meaningful ways. Acceptance helps release denial, allowing you to solve problems creatively to find useful solutions to resolve issues in your life.

I acknowledge the truth, accept it for what it is, and love myself unconditionally.

MEDITATION

One of the biggest problems with denial is that, on a conscious level, you probably don't realize you're in denial. However, on a subconscious level, you probably know you are in denial about something. So before you can reach acceptance, you must acknowledge that which you are denying. This meditation helps you reveal your denial, acknowledge it, and reach acceptance. Lie comfortably on your back with your eyes closed, breathing normally. Ask yourself, "What am I denying?" Then, focus on your third eye and watch what arises. When you have a clear picture of what you are denying, speak the mantra, surrounding yourself with healing white light.

REMEDY #1: PURPLE & GREEN FLUORITE CHAKRA WORK

To facilitate the meditation, use two pieces of fluorite—one purple and one green. Place the purple fluorite on your third eye chakra to facilitate insight and the green fluorite on your heart chakra to facilitate unconditional love and acceptance. Proceed with the meditation. (You can replace the purple and green fluorite with two pieces of rainbow fluorite that have just the purple and green in them, if you don't specifically have one piece of purple and one green.)

REMEDY #2: RAINBOW FLUORITE & CLEAR QUARTZ CHAKRA WORK

For this meditation, use a single piece of rainbow fluorite that has blue, green, and purple in it. Lie on your back with the rainbow fluorite on your throat chakra and the clear quartz on your crown chakra. The blue in the fluorite will help stimulate speaking your truth, which is essential for releasing denial and finding acceptance. The clear quartz will amplify spiritual energy, providing you with strength and support from the Divine. Visualize light coming into your crown chakra through the quartz and into your throat chakra from the fluorite. Run the energy up into your third eye chakra and down into your heart chakra. Repeat the mantra as you do this for 5 to 10 minutes.

Despair & Hope

Despair arises when all hope seems lost. Finding even the smallest sliver of hope during times of despair can ignite healing, keeping you from becoming paralyzed by your despair and enabling you to make the choice to move forward with your life. When you feel despair, you can take steps to overcome the bleakness and reignite your hope.

Nothing is permanent. All things change. I have hope for a positive future.

MEDITATION

Make a list of all of the things you'd like your life to be, and turn each into a positive affirmation. Every day, choose three positive affirmations and repeat each one three times, starting and ending your session with the mantra.

REMEDY #1: ALEXANDRITE & TOURMALINE

As you state your affirmations, hold a piece of black tourmaline in your giving (dominant) hand and a piece of alexandrite in your receiving (nondominant) hand. The tourmaline will absorb your despair, while the alexandrite will impart hope. Be sure to cleanse and charge these crystals after every session, because despair is a very heavy energy that will quickly fill your crystal.

REMEDY #2: CITRINE & SMOKY QUARTZ GRID

Make a simple line grid with citrine and smoky quartz. Place a piece of smoky quartz of any shape in the center, with two citrine points on either side of it, pointing toward you. Place the grid in a place where you spend a lot of time, or next to your bed. The smoky quartz will absorb and transform the negative energy of despair into positive energy, while the citrine will impart hope, directed through the points of the crystals. Cleanse and charge your crystals daily.

Fear & Courage

Everyone feels fear from time to time; it's a natural human response. Courage in the face of fear means acting constructively, no matter how afraid you are. Acts of courage don't need to be big or bold to matter. Sometimes, courage comes from having the strength to be who you are in the face of fear of rejection. Whether your acts of courage are large or small, overcoming fear to make positive change is a tremendous act of bravery.

I have the strength to face all circumstances; I have the courage to act and move forward.

MEDITATION

Fear is a root chakra issue, while courage is a solar plexus chakra issue. To overcome fear with courage, lie on your back with your eyes closed, breathing normally. Allow yourself to feel your fear, noting any sensations in your root chakra. Now, move your attention to your solar plexus chakra. Visualize the golden light of that chakra glowing strongly. Move your fear from the root chakra up into the solar plexus chakra, allowing the golden light to overtake it. Continue meditating for at least 10 minutes.

REMEDY #1: GARNET & AQUAMARINE

Garnet helps alleviate fear, while aquamarine enables you to act courageously. Hold the garnet in your giving (dominant) hand and the aquamarine in your receiving (nondominant) hand. Sit quietly with your eyes closed, feeling your fear flow into the garnet and courage flow into you from the aquamarine. Be sure to cleanse and charge both stones regularly if you are in a situation that requires a lot of courage.

REMEDY #2: TIGERS EYE & BLOODSTONE CHAKRA WORK

Place a piece of yellow tigers eye on your solar plexus chakra and a piece of bloodstone on your root chakra as you do the meditation.

 TIP: For courage in certain aspects of your life, use a stone for that chakra as well. For example, if you are afraid of speaking your truth and need courage to do so, use the tigers eye and bloodstone, but add a throat chakra stone such as lapis lazuli. For overcoming fear and having courage in love, add a heart chakra stone such as rose quartz.

Goals & Motivation

Setting goals can help you achieve the things you desire in life, but sometimes motivation slips. Engaging in the thoughts, words, and deeds necessary to meet your short-term and long-term goals requires motivation to keep moving forward. However, even when we're steadily progressing toward meeting our goals, life often gets in the way and suddenly we have lost our drive to move forward. Working with these two areas in combination can help you keep your eyes on the prize and continue to take positive steps in that direction.

I maintain motivation to meet my goals.

MEDITATION

Write down your goals as affirmations, wording them as if you have already achieved those goals. For example, if your goal is to run a marathon, you might affirm, "I am grateful I have completed my marathon successfully and feel happy and healthy." Each morning upon waking, repeat each of your affirmations three times. Then, close your eyes and visualize yourself doing what you need to do each day to take steps to achieve your goal.

REMEDY #1: MULTI-STONE GRID

This square grid requires five stones, all that help focus on different aspects of goals and motivation. Start with a clear quartz point or cluster in the center for amplification. Around the quartz point, arrange a carnelian for motivation, yellow tigers eye for self-confidence, obsidian for self-control, and sodalite for integrity. Form a square around the center clear quartz, and place the grid on your bedside table. Cleanse and recharge the stones once or twice a week.

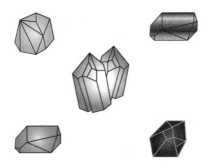

REMEDY #2: AMETHYST & CARNELIAN

Before going to sleep, lie on your back with a piece of amethyst on your third eye chakra. Ask, "What are my goals?" Focus on your third eye, watching what arises. Now, write the goals on a piece of paper and wrap the paper around a carnelian crystal. Place the wrapped carnelian under your pillow. The amethyst helps clarify your thinking, while the carnelian provides energy and motivation to take steps to achieve your goals upon waking.

Grief & Comfort

When we grieve, we long for comfort. However, during intense grieving, comfort may be difficult to find, no matter how much others try to offer solace. Finding a source of comfort within yourself may be your most effective way of assisting your grief. In this case, comfort comes from your higher self, as well as from a source such as your spirit guides, lost loved ones, or any deity in which you believe.

I receive comfort from my higher self to ease my grief.

MEDITATION

Sit quietly with your eyes closed, breathing deeply. Say to yourself, "I thank my higher power for bringing me comfort in my time of grief." Allow yourself to feel warmth and comfort entering your body from the universe, surrounding you in a loving white light. Speak the mantra as you sit, allowing yourself to be embraced by the light for as long as you need.

REMEDY #1: SMOKY QUARTZ & APACHE TEARS

Hold a piece of smoky quartz in your giving (dominant) hand and a piece of Apache tears in your receiving (nondominant) hand. The smoky quartz will receive, absorb, and transform your grief, while the Apache tears will impart comforting energy. You can do this during the meditation, or anytime throughout the day when your grief threatens to overwhelm you. Be sure to cleanse and charge the crystals daily, because the intense emotions will quickly fill them with energy.

REMEDY #2: AQUAMARINE & SELENITE

Use aquamarine to facilitate emotional release from painful emotions and selenite to seek comfort from a higher power. Hold the aquamarine in your giving (dominant) hand and the selenite in your receiving (nondominant) hand, allowing your emotions to flow into the aquamarine and the peace and comfort from the selenite to flow into you. Continue for at least 10 minutes or until you feel a sense of comfort and a lessening of your grief.

Grounding & Spiritual Protection

Healers, light workers, energy workers, people who use psychic intuition, people who are highly empathic, and people in psychically charged atmospheres can benefit from this combination of remedies. Grounding is especially important because it keeps you firmly rooted to Earth. Adding spiritual protection can keep you safe from any negative energy, which is important because these types of work tend to leave you quite open to others' energetic influences.

I am grounded, centered, and surrounded by a white light of protection.

MEDITATION

Sit comfortably in a chair with your feet on the floor, eyes closed, and breathing normally. Put both hands over your belly button. State the mantra. Now, visualize a silver cord of light extending from the bottom of your feet into the Earth. Anchor your cord in the center of the Earth and picture a pink light moving up the cord and into your belly. Feel the pink light turn into a warm ball in your belly, growing warm under your hands and moving into them. Now, extend your hands to your sides, palms facing up. Release the light from your hands into a circle all around you as you push the pink light from your core outward, surrounding you completely. Repeat the mantra 10 times.

REMEDY #1: BLACK TOURMALINE & CLEAR QUARTZ

Tourmaline is both a grounding and a protective stone, while clear quartz calls in the Divine. I always carry tourmaline and clear quartz when I am doing energy work, cleansing and recharging the crystals as soon as I have completed the work. The quartz amplifies the grounding and protective properties of the black tourmaline. Use these two stones together—black tourmaline in your giving (dominant) hand and quartz in your receiving (nondominant) hand—when you feel you need grounding and protection.

REMEDY #2: POLISHED HEMATITE & SELENITE

Polished hematite has a reflective surface that can reflect negative energy away from you. At the same time, its deep red to black color makes it a root chakra stone that helps you ground yourself. Wear a polished hematite ring for grounding and protection, making sure you cleanse the ring as soon as you have finished doing your energy work. Use selenite to call protection from a higher source, as well as to cleanse the ring as needed. If you do a lot of energy work, you may wish to keep a few different rings in rotation.

 TIP: A hematite ring will break when it has used up all its grounding and protective energy or become saturated with negative energy. Don't be alarmed if this happens, as it is quite common. It merely signals that it is time to use a different ring. Be sure to throw away the pieces of the ring. Don't store the pieces with your other crystals, because the hematite is loaded with the negative energy it has absorbed.

Guilt & Shame

Guilt and shame are two sides of the same coin. These all-too-common self-destructive emotions offer an opportunity to better yourself even as they present challenges. While they serve as a compass to help you, when you internalize them and allow them to become part of your self-image, they can prevent you from moving forward with your life in a healthy manner.

I acknowledge my actions that led to my guilt. I release any lingering shame.

MEDITATION

Meditate with a root chakra stone, such as a garnet, in either of your hands. Focus on this chakra as you meditate. Take a deep breath in and say, "I acknowledge my actions that led to my guilt." As you exhale, picture your shame flowing out through your root chakra and dissipating into the universe while repeating, "I release any lingering shame." Do this for at least 10 minutes or until you feel a release.

REMEDY #1: AMAZONITE & GARNET CHAKRA WORK

Shame and guilt are root chakra issues. When our actions warrant these feelings, however, our throat (integrity) chakra comes into play, as well. Lie on your back on the floor or a bed. Place amazonite on your throat chakra and a garnet on your root chakra. Close your eyes and feel the energy flow between the two chakras, staying in place for 10 to 15 minutes. Allow yourself to flow with any emotions that arise, feeling and releasing them fully.

REMEDY #2: PERIDOT & CITRINE

Sit comfortably. Hold a peridot in your giving (dominant) hand and close your eyes. Visualize your guilt and shame as dark shadows in your body and see them lifting away from you and dissipating into the universe. Fill your body with healing white light. When you have completed the visualization, sit quietly holding citrine in your receiving (nondominant) hand to build self-confidence, with your attention focused on your solar plexus. Do this for five minutes.

Insecurity & Self-Confidence

Your security forms in your root chakra, while self-confidence arises from the solar plexus chakra. The two often go hand in hand; if you've never felt secure, it is difficult to have any type of self-confidence. To strengthen your self-confidence, you must first take care of any safety and security issues you have. A person's higher-level needs cannot be addressed until the lower-level needs are met.

I am safe, secure, and confident in myself and my life.

MEDITATION

Meditate to strengthen your root chakra and your solar plexus chakra. Lie on your back with your eyes closed, breathing normally. Visualize a red swirling light in your root chakra and a yellow swirling light in your solar plexus chakra. Run energy from one chakra to the other. Do this for at least 10 minutes, repeating the mantra as you do.

REMEDY #1: RED & YELLOW TIGERS EYE

I love tigers eye as a self-confidence stone—to me, it just feels so powerfully self-affirming. I have it in all colors, and they are among my favorite stones. In this case, use red tigers eye on your root chakra and yellow tigers eye on your solar plexus chakra as you do the meditation.

REMEDY #2: SARDONYX & SUNSTONE

Sardonyx in either red or black is a great dual-purpose stone. It helps clear up safety issues associated with the root chakra, and it also serves as a confidence booster. Sunstone will also boost your self-esteem. Carry sardonyx and sunstone in your pants pocket so it is near both of these chakras when you are feeling insecure and need a confidence boost.

TIP: Any root chakra stone can help you clear away insecurity, while any solar plexus chakra stone can increase self-confidence. Try different combinations of red or black root chakra stones and golden or yellow solar plexus chakra stones to see which helps you the most. You can use them in the meditation or carry them with you. If you hold them in your hands, always hold the aspect you'd like to receive (in this case, confidence) in your receiving (nondominant) hand, and always hold the aspect you'd like to dispel in your giving (dominant) hand.

Inspiration & Creativity

Even the most creative people among us occasionally feel blocked in our creative pursuits. That is when we are especially in need of a spark of inspiration to stoke our creativity. But even if you aren't experiencing a creative block or aren't a particularly creative person, finding creative inspiration can result in positive benefits along your life's path.

I am inspired by my higher self and express my creativity in all aspects of my life.

MEDITATION

Inspiration comes from your crown chakra, where you receive inspiration from the Source, as well as from your third eye chakra, which is the seat of inspiration and insight from your higher self. Creativity forms in the sacral chakra. Incorporating all these chakras into a single meditation can help stimulate the flow of ideas and inspiration from higher chakras down to your chakra of creativity. Sit comfortably with your eyes closed, breathing normally. Visualize a white light coming from above and entering through your crown chakra. Bring the energy into your third eye chakra, mixing the white light with the violet or indigo of the third eye. Next, bring that energy down through your chakras to your sacral chakra, where it mixes with the orange energy you find there. As you do so, repeat the mantra for at least 10 minutes.

REMEDY #1: AMETHYST & AMETRINE GRID

Amethyst is a crystal of both the crown and third eye chakras, which brings inspiration, while citrine is a stone of creativity. To spark creativity while you sleep, place a small ametrine grid on your bedside table. Place a piece of amethyst in the center of the grid, and then add three ametrine pieces in a triangle around the center stone. Make sure one of the triangle points directly points at your head to direct the energy your way. (If you do not have ametrine, you can use citrine instead.)

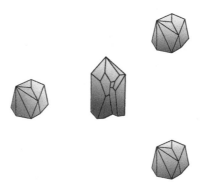

REMEDY #2: CITRINE & ORANGE CALCITE

Citrine can help you open your mind, allowing inspiration to enter. Orange calcite draws up the creativity from the sacral chakra and combines it with inspiration from a higher source. Sit quietly for 5 to 10 minutes with a piece of citrine in your receiving (nondominant) hand, focusing on your solar plexus chakra. Next, perform the meditation while holding a piece of orange calcite in your receiving hand.

Loneliness & Contentment

Many people believe that the opposite of loneliness is love, but it is really contentment. Sometimes in life, we are unable to find the love we desire with another human being. The feeling of loneliness may exist so that we continue to reach out to others, or it may urge us to commune with ourselves, our spirit, and the Source. Finding contentment in your life—no matter your relationship status or how many or few people are in your life—is a significant way to address the loneliness you may feel.

I am at peace and content in my own company.

MEDITATION

Sit comfortably with your eyes closed, breathing normally. Visualize yourself sitting alone in a space, where there is nothing there but you. Now, speak the mantra and allow light to come from above and inside of you, surrounding you in white light and love. Do this for at least 10 minutes.

REMEDY #1: AMETHYST, CITRINE, & ROSE QUARTZ

Amethyst connects you to spirit and your higher self, citrine enhances your enjoyment of your own company, and rose quartz enhances unconditional love for self and others. Do the meditation with the amethyst and citrine in your receiving (nondominant) hand and the rose quartz in your giving (dominant) hand, which you press gently to your heart chakra.

REMEDY #2: RUBY IN FUCHSITE

Ruby is another stone that fosters contentment, while fuchsite is a heart stone that fosters self-love and positive relationships. The two come together in ruby in fuchsite, making it the perfect stone for this combination of issues. Place a piece of ruby in fuchsite under your pillow at night, cleansing and recharging the crystal each morning. You can also use separate pieces of ruby and fuchsite, placed together, for this remedy.

Opening the Heart & Relationships

Every time you interact with another person, you are in some type of a relationship with them. While many people tend to think of relationships as being only with friends, family, and colleagues, in truth, you are in a relationship of some type with every person you encounter. Having an open and loving heart can help improve every relationship that enters your life— from your significant other all the way to the person who serves you at the deli counter. Opening your heart facilitates positive interactions.

My heart is open to unconditionally loving relationships and interactions.

MEDITATION

With everyone you meet, no matter how brief the interaction, imagine a green light flowing from your heart chakra to theirs and from their heart chakra to yours. If this is difficult for you to do, practice it by sitting quietly and visualizing yourself going about your day, encountering people, and seeing this exchange of open-hearted love take place.

REMEDY #1: ROSE QUARTZ & LAPIS LAZULI CHAKRA WORK

Lie on your back with your eyes closed. Place a piece of rose quartz on your heart chakra and a piece of lapis lazuli on your throat chakra. Visualize energy flowing between the two chakras. The rose quartz will open your heart, while the lapis lazuli will facilitate communication and help you have truthful and honest relationships. Lie this way for 10 minutes.

REMEDY #2: ROSE QUARTZ & CITRINE CHAKRA WORK

Sometimes the person to whom you need to open your heart is yourself. This chakra meditation focuses on the solar plexus chakra, which is where you build self-esteem, and the heart chakra, where you find unconditional love. Use a piece of rose quartz and a piece of citrine for this meditation. Lie comfortably on your back with the rose quartz on your heart chakra and the citrine on your solar plexus chakra. Close your eyes and visualize each chakra opening, with energy flowing freely between them and throughout your body. Continue your meditation for at least 10 minutes.

Releasing Negativity & Increasing Positive Energy

The Law of Attraction states that whatever you put out into the universe, you receive back. Therefore, if you're caught in a spiral of negativity, you are creating energetic circumstances in which more negativity can come back to you. This can be a very difficult cycle to get out of, unless you actively work to increase the positive energy in your life. If you're stuck in a negative pattern, it's essential not to dwell on the negativity and give it more energy, but rather focus on generating positive energy to turn things around.

I am filled with positive energy, which brings positive things into my life.

MEDITATION

Sit comfortably with your eyes closed, breathing deeply. As you exhale, imagine your negative energy as a dark cloud leaving your body and dissolving into a white light that surrounds you. As you inhale, visualize the positive white light entering and filling you as you repeat the mantra. Do this for at least 10 minutes every day.

REMEDY #1: IOLITE & BLACK TOURMALINE

Iolite is a beautiful watery-blue crystal that attracts positive energy, while black tourmaline absorbs negativity. Do the meditation while holding the black tourmaline in your giving (dominant) hand and the iolite in your receiving (nondominant) hand. Be sure to cleanse and charge the crystals a few times each week to keep them working well.

REMEDY #2: MOLDAVITE & AMBER

I'm a sucker for any crystal that does more than one thing at a time, which is why I think moldavite is so perfect for transforming energy. It is a crystal of transformation, so it can turn the energy of any situation from negative to positive. This is a great stone to use when you feel like you're caught in a negative spiral. Amber is a stone of happiness and joy, so it increases positive energy. Do the meditation with moldavite in your giving (dominant) hand and amber in your receiving (nondominant) hand for 10 minutes, noticing how the energy going into the moldavite transforms and returns to you with positive vibes, while the amber adds positive energy and happiness from the receiving hand. Cleanse the stones daily if you're in an intensely negative cycle, or a few times a week otherwise.

Resentment & Letting Go

When you resent someone, you hold both you and that other person captive spiritually and emotionally. It can negatively affect future relationships, as well. Learning to let go of resentment can heal relationships, or it can provide you both with release, allowing you to move forward with your lives, whether together or apart. Some relationships can't be healed, even after letting go of resentment, and that's okay. What's important is that you both learned the lessons you needed from the relationship and that you have released each other into a positive and healthy future.

I release [name the person] from anger and resentment and bless [him/her] for a positive future.

MEDITATION

Sit comfortably with your eyes closed, breathing normally. Visualize the person toward whom you hold resentment, and picture your resentment as heavy chains surrounding that person. Now, send loving light from your heart to that person, watching as the love breaks the chains around him or her. Surround the person entirely with light as you repeat the mantra for at least 10 minutes.

REMEDY #1: CARNELIAN & MOSS AGATE

Red carnelian can help you release resentment, while moss agate helps with both resentment and letting go. This green stone is a good choice for the heart chakra, which allows you to love in the face of anger or resentment. Moss agate can also help you let go of bitterness and anger. Do the meditation while holding a piece of moss agate in your receiving (nondominant) hand and a piece of carnelian in your giving (dominant) hand.

REMEDY #2: BLACK TOURMALINE & AMBER

Sometimes resentment and bitterness are earned because one or both partners bring a lot of toxic energy into the relationship. In this case, it is even more important to let go of those emotions. Black tourmaline can help by absorbing the negative energy created by the relationship itself and helping you release both yourself and the other person. Meditate with a piece of black tourmaline in your giving (dominant) hand for 10 minutes daily for at least a week, focusing on releasing the resentment or negative feelings you have and allowing it to flow into the black tourmaline. Cleanse and recharge the tourmaline as soon as you finish each meditation session. Follow the meditation with five minutes of holding amber in your receiving (nondominant) hand to foster warm feelings and happiness.

 TIP: Sometimes the best way to heal a relationship is to step away from it, letting it go. Resentment often builds in a relationship that no longer mutually serves both persons' paths in life. But acknowledge your time together was beneficial to both. This can help you separate and let go with gratitude for the help you provided each other along life's path.

Stress & Peace

Too much stress in your life can rob you of your sense of peacefulness. Finding a place of peace within, however, can provide refuge from unavoidable stress, allowing you some respite during stressful times. We all have a peaceful place in us where we can go and recharge, no matter what's going on in our lives. Locating your source of peace can help you keep stress at bay.

I release all stress and enter my place of peace.

MEDITATION

Sit quietly with your eyes closed, breathing deeply. Focus all your energy within, locating a quiet space inside you. As you focus on this peaceful place, inhale peace and exhale stress while repeating the mantra. Stay in the meditation for at least 10 minutes.

REMEDY #1: ONYX & SELENITE

Black onyx absorbs negative energy, while selenite has a very peaceful energy. Holding selenite or even gazing at it can help you reach a more calm and peaceful state. During times of stress, keep onyx and selenite with you. When you feel stressed, hold the onyx in your giving (dominant) hand, breathing deeply and allowing it to absorb your stress. Then, hold selenite in your receiving (nondominant) hand and gaze deeply into its depths as you take deep breaths and repeat the mantra 10 times.

REMEDY #2: OBSIDIAN & BLUE CALCITE

Obsidian can calm and absorb negative energy, while blue calcite can help ease physical signs of stress, soothing your senses and allowing you to find inner peace. Hold the obsidian in your giving (dominant) hand and the blue calcite in your receiving (nondominant) hand as you do the meditation.

 TIP: If you work in a very stressful environment, keep a piece of selenite on your desk. One good choice that you can find in many crystal shops is a selenite tower on a lighted base. The base changes the color of the light, making the selenite glow in different hues. Watching the selenite glow with changing colors can release stress and increase your feelings of peace.

6

Crystal Profiles

Here you'll find profiles of 99 crystals to help familiarize you with their origins, colors, and primary uses. These profiles also specify each crystal's chakra association for those who wish to integrate chakra work into their crystals practice. Finally, each entry notes recommended placement for the crystal to maximize its vibrational power.

Agate

Agate is a form of quartz and chalcedony. It is a translucent, banded stone that comes in a variety of colors and forms. You can find many different types, cuts, and shapes of agates, including smooth rounded stones, polished stones, rough stones, and polished cross sections, or slabs. Many commercially available agates have been dyed to enhance the color characteristics of the stone.

ORIGIN

Australia, Brazil, Czech Republic, India, Mexico, Morocco, United States

COLORS

Blue, green, brown, yellow, pink, white, orange, black, purple, gray, red

PRIMARY USES

Enhances emotional balance and healing, balances yin and yang, promotes emotional calmness, increases self-confidence, improves focus and concentration, helps overcome bitterness, heals resentment (other uses depend on color)

CHAKRA

Heart, root

PLACEMENT

Place on the appropriate chakras, hold in either hand, wear as jewelry, carry in a pocket

BLUE LACE

Agate

This soft blue agate has mesmerizing white or gray bands running through it. It's a very pretty stone with a light translucent quality and a high shine when polished. It is a relatively hard crystal.

ORIGIN

Africa (particularly South Africa), Australia, Brazil

COLORS

Sky blue to violet blue with white and gray bands

PRIMARY USES

Promotes a sense of calm, facilitates calm and truthful communication, helps with public speaking, promotes tranquility, helps lessen deep negative emotions, facilitates communication with spiritual beings

CHAKRA

Third eye, throat

PLACEMENT

Place on or touching the appropriate chakras, hold in the receiving (nondominant) hand for calm or the giving (dominant) hand for communicating truthfully or gently, wear as jewelry (particularly necklace or earrings), carry in a pocket, place at a lectern for public speaking, keep in meditation area

MOSS

Agate

Once you see moss agate, you'll understand how it got its name. This agate is the color of moss, with variations in color from light to deep green and flecks of white, brown, gray, or black. It is a translucent stone.

ORIGIN

Australia, Brazil, Czech Republic, India, Mexico, Morocco, United States

COLORS

Green

PRIMARY USES

Fosters appreciation of nature, improves gardening abilities, supports new beginnings, attracts prosperity, encourages love of all types

CHAKRA

Heart

PLACEMENT

Place on or touching the heart chakra, hold in either hand, keep in wallet or cash box, place around plants or in garden shed, carry in a shirt or jacket pocket

Alexandrite

When cut into facets, this unique crystal changes color from bluish green or green to purple, depending on the position of the stone and how it is lit. This color change makes the stone highly desirable, but also quite scarce. Much of the alexandrite you will find available may be manufactured from Austrian crystal—beautiful in its own right, but without any healing properties. The mineral got its name from its use in Czarist Russia and is named after Czar Alexander II.

ORIGIN

Brazil, Russia, Sri Lanka

COLORS

Green to bluish green, changing to purple to raspberry

PRIMARY USES

Boosts self-esteem, intensifies positive emotions, enhances confidence, promotes optimism, increases joy, brings luck, facilitates connection to higher self, improves intuition

CHAKRA

Heart, third eye, crown

PLACEMENT

Place on the appropriate chakra, wear as jewelry, hold in receiving (nondominant) hand, carry in a pocket

Amazonite

Amazonite is a member of the feldspar family with a blue-green/ turquoise color and a slightly iridescent luster. It is a relatively soft stone, so it scratches and dings easily. Therefore, it's best to carry amazonite by itself or wrapped in a cloth so other rocks don't scratch it. Don't use water or salt to cleanse this crystal.

ORIGIN

Australia, Brazil, Canada, Namibia, Russia, United States, Zimbabwe

COLORS

Green, aqua

PRIMARY USES

Provides protection against electromagnetic energies, calms and soothes, promotes peace, relieves stress, helps balance yin and yang, promotes personal truth, opens the heart and promotes love, triggers intuition

CHAKRA

Throat, heart

PLACEMENT

Place directly on the appropriate chakra, use on the third eye for intuition, hold in the receiving (nondominant) hand for peace, hold in the giving (dominant) hand to absorb stress, carry in a pocket, wear as jewelry (particularly necklace and earrings)

Amber

Although not technically a crystal, amber is used extensively in crystal healing. It is actually fossilized tree resin. The best amber comes from the Baltic region. It may often have small impurities in it, including bubbles, pieces of matter, or even fossilized insects. Don't use water or salt to cleanse this crystal.

ORIGIN

Dominican Republic, Germany, Great Britain, Italy, Poland, Romania, Russia

COLORS

Golden yellow to deep honey brown

PRIMARY USES

Eases pain, clears negativity, cleanses chakras and auras, cleanses energy from the environment, enhances memory, promotes peace and trust, relieves stress

CHAKRA

Solar plexus, throat

PLACEMENT

Wear as jewelry (necklace, bracelet, earrings), carry in a pocket, hold in receiving (nondominant) hand to receive positive energy

Amethyst

Amethyst is a quartz crystal and a semiprecious gemstone. Its name is a derivation of the Greek word *amethustos*, meaning "not drunk." Throughout history, people have considered it to be a stone that prevents intoxication and helps support sobriety.

ORIGIN

Brazil, Canada, East Africa, Great Britain, India, Mexico, Russia, Sri Lanka, United States

COLORS

Purple

PRIMARY USES

Enhances intuition and inner sight, supports sobriety, treats insomnia, promotes restful sleep, enhances psychic abilities, supports connection to the spiritual realm and higher self

CHAKRA

Third eye, crown

PLACEMENT

Place directly on or touching the appropriate chakra, wear as any type of jewelry (particularly necklace and earrings), carry in a pocket, hold in the receiving (nondominant) hand, place under the pillow or on bedside table, keep in meditation area

Ametrine

Ametrine is a quartz crystal that is a natural combination of amethyst and citrine, resulting in a lovely and unusual bicolored stone.

ORIGIN

Brazil, Canada, East Africa, Great Britain, India, Mexico, Russia, Sri Lanka, United States

COLORS

Purple and yellow

PRIMARY USES

Combines powerful qualities of both amethyst and citrine, promotes prosperity, improves self-esteem, facilitates connection with higher consciousness, enhances spiritual and mental clarity, cleanses the aura, releases negativity

CHAKRA

Third eye, solar plexus, crown

PLACEMENT

Place on or touching the appropriate chakra, wear as any type of jewelry (particularly necklace and earrings), carry in a pocket, keep in the prosperity corner of your home, hold in your receiving (nondominant) hand, keep in your wallet or cashbox, keep in meditation area, place next to the bed or under a pillow or mattress

Angelite

Angelite is a type of celestite that forms over thousands of years of being under tremendous pressure. Typically, you'll find this light blue-gray stone as a polished rounded rock, but you may also find slices of it. The stone has white striations throughout, particularly in the cross-sections.

ORIGIN

Great Britain, Libya, Mexico, Peru, Poland

COLORS

Grayish blue with white

PRIMARY USES

Promotes awareness, helps connect with higher consciousness, encourages peace, supports contact with higher beings, enables one to live and speak with integrity, promotes compassion

CHAKRA

Throat, third eye, crown

PLACEMENT

Place on or touching the appropriate chakra, touch to base of feet for chakra cleansing, wear as jewelry (particularly necklace or earrings), carry in a pocket, hold in the receiving (nondominant) hand, keep in meditation area

Apache Tears

Apache tears are smoothly rounded pieces of obsidian, which is a type of dark volcanic glass. They are warm and smooth to the touch and translucent when held up to a light source. They are reasonably soft and may scratch easily, so you might want to keep them wrapped in a cloth and away from direct contact with other stones. Don't use water or salt to cleanse this crystal.

ORIGIN

All over the world

COLORS

Dark gray to black

PRIMARY USES

Provides support for grief, allows sadness to pass through, absorbs negativity, enhances grounding, triggers emotional healing, provides spiritual protection, offers protection against negative emotions (both yours and others'), helps in recovery from abuse

CHAKRA

Root

PLACEMENT

Place on or touching the root chakra, hold in the giving (dominant) hand, carry in pants pocket, keep in a particular place for protection from negativity, carry to funerals or other grief-related occasions

Apatite

Apatite is a phosphate mineral. It is typically blue, although you can find it in other colors, such as yellow, but that is fairly rare. It is a brittle stone, so it may break easily if you drop it. For this reason, treat apatite with care and use caution when it is in contact with other stones.

ORIGIN

Mexico, Norway, Russia, United States

COLORS

Blue, yellow, white, gray, green, purple/violet

PRIMARY USES

Enhances self-expression, facilitates inspiration for ideas and creativity, promotes energy to aid in manifesting one's desires, improves motivation

CHAKRA

Throat, third eye

PLACEMENT

Place on or touching the appropriate chakra, hold in either hand, use anywhere on the body it is needed, carry in a pocket, wear as jewelry (particularly necklace and earrings), bring to a meeting room or elsewhere to facilitate communication, keep on desk to spur creative thought, keep in meditation area to help manifest affirmations and visualizations

Aquamarine

This crystal has the name and the color of the ocean, and sailors used it for centuries to promote safe sea journeys and prevent drowning. Aquamarine is a variety of beryl, and it is often used to make beautiful gemstone jewelry, prized for its stunning blue-green color.

ORIGIN

Brazil, Ireland, Mexico, Middle East, Russia, United States, Zimbabwe

COLORS

Bluish green/greenish blue

PRIMARY USES

Provides courage, offers protection against negative energies, promotes safe travel, helps with phobias, lessens anxiety and fear, promotes speaking the truth, cleanses and strengthens the aura, overcomes judgment, aids in calming and relieving stress

CHAKRA

Heart, third eye, throat

PLACEMENT

Wear as jewelry (particularly a necklace or earrings), place on the appropriate chakras, carry in a pocket, hold in the receiving (nondominant) hand, use anywhere on the body it's needed, tuck into carry-on luggage for safe travel

Aragonite

This stone is a crystalline form of calcium carbonate, which also occurs in coral, limestone, and other rock formations. It is named after the village of Molina de Aragon in Spain. It is a relatively soft mineral, so care must be taken to prevent damage. Don't use water or salt to cleanse this crystal.

ORIGIN

Great Britain, Slovakia, Spain

COLORS

White, brown, yellow, green

PRIMARY USES

Aids grounding, fosters acceptance, generates emotional balance, fights stress, soothes anxiety, lessens resentment, aids concentration

CHAKRA

Root, solar plexus, crown

PLACEMENT

Place on or touching the appropriate chakras, hold in the hands while grounding, keep in meditation area, carry in pants pocket, keep at desk if you have a stressful job

BLUE

Aventurine

A lovely royal blue color, possibly tinged with gray, blue aventurine also contains quartz inclusions. The name aventurine comes from the term "aventurescence," an optical effect seen in stones with a highly reflective surface.

ORIGIN

Brazil, China, India, Italy, Nepal, Russia, Tibet

COLORS

Blue gray to blue

PRIMARY USES

Increases psychic awareness and insight, promotes personal integrity, improves communication, calms stress, improves self-discipline, supports the ability to overcome bad habits

CHAKRA

Third eye, throat

PLACEMENT

Place on or touching the appropriate chakras, hold in either hand, carry in a pocket, keep in an area to promote calmness or enhance communications

Aventurine

Green aventurine has a bright green color with white and/or gray banding. The crystal is opaque with a luster to it. It is a form of quartz, and the green color comes from fuchsite.

ORIGIN

Brazil, China, India, Italy, Nepal, Russia, Tibet

COLORS

Light to vivid green

PRIMARY USES

Increases love, supports prosperity and abundance, facilitates healing, introduces new friendship

CHAKRA

Heart

PLACEMENT

Place on or touching the heart chakra, wear as jewelry (particularly a necklace), carry in a pocket, hold in the receiving (nondominant) hand for receiving friendship or the giving (dominant) hand for giving friendship, keep in the prosperity corner of home or room

ORANGE

Aventurine

This orange stone has a light sheen. It may be a brownish orange or a pure orange. It is lightly transparent, and you may notice flecks of darker or lighter orange within the gemstone.

ORIGIN

Brazil, China, India, Italy, Nepal, Russia, Tibet

COLORS

Orange

PRIMARY USES

Promotes luck, helps foster new beginnings, instills an adventurous spirit, promotes perseverance, strengthens resolve, helps establish self-will and self-control

CHAKRA

Sacral, root

PLACEMENT

Place on or touching the appropriate chakras, hold in either hand, carry in pants pocket, wear as jewelry (particularly rings and bracelets)

Azurite

As the name suggests, azurite is a beautiful deep blue (azure) crystal containing flecks of gold, green, or yellow. It is a relatively soft crystal, so you need to take care when you carry it or use it with other stones, to avoid damage. It is often found within copper deposits and may be a rough stone or a polished crystal.

ORIGIN

Australia, Chile, Egypt, France, Peru, Russia, United States

COLORS

Deep blue

PRIMARY USES

Opens the third eye, supports communication with higher self, strengthens intuition, supports enlightenment, aids psychic development, helps resolve deep negative emotions such as grief or stress, enhances communication, fosters personal integrity

CHAKRA

Third eye, throat

PLACEMENT

Place on or touching the appropriate chakras, hold in the receiving (nondominant) hand, wear as jewelry (particularly necklace or earrings), keep in meditation area, carry to funerals or other emotional events

Bloodstone

Also known as heliotrope, bloodstone is so named because it is believed to help purify the blood and fight blood disorders. The stone is green with red flecks and is actually chalcedony flecked with iron oxide. The combination of colors makes it a good stone when you are working with the root and heart chakras together.

ORIGIN

Australia, Brazil, China, India, Russia

COLORS

Green with red spots

PRIMARY USES

Supports grounding, opens the heart, promotes development of personal power, enhances courage, releases fear, fosters strength of mind

CHAKRA

Root, heart

PLACEMENT

Place on or touching the appropriate chakras, hold in either hand (receiving, or nondominant, hand for courage; giving, or dominant, hand for fear), carry in a pocket, wear as any type of jewelry, carry for courage in the face of fear

Boji Stones

Boji Stones aren't much to look at, but many people feel they are powerful crystals. They are rounded brown to gray rocks, typically pyrite and marcasite, with a rough or smooth surface, and they always come in pairs that consist of a male and a female stone. The name Boji Stone is a trademarked name; you may also find these stones under the name Kansas Pop Rocks.

ORIGIN

Kansas

COLORS

Brown, dark gray, black

PRIMARY USES

Balances energy, recharges the aura, aligns the chakras

CHAKRA

All chakras

PLACEMENT

Lie on back and place one stone on head and one touching soles of the feet, hold one stone in each hand, wear around the neck

BLUE

Calcite

Blue is one of the many colors of calcite, a stone formed from calcium carbonate. The surface of calcite looks almost chalky, and the blue color tends to be grayish blue. All colors of calcite are relatively soft, so you need to take care when using them around other stones or carrying them in a pocket. Don't use water or salt to cleanse this crystal.

ORIGIN

Belgium, Brazil,
Czech Republic, Great Britain,
Iceland, Peru, Russia,
United States

COLORS

Blue

PRIMARY USES

Calms and soothes, promotes relaxation, enhances intuition, improves focus and memory, improves communication

CHAKRA

Third eye, throat

PLACEMENT

Place on or touching the appropriate chakras, hold in either hand, carry in a shirt pocket, keep in an area to promote calmness and relaxation, keep in a conference room to support communication, place near the family dining table to support communication, keep in the bedroom for relaxation

Calcite

Green calcite in its rough form has a waxy surface with a slight luster. It comes in various shades of green from medium to dark with white striations. When tumbled and polished, it loses its waxy appearance and has a high luster.

ORIGIN

Belgium, Brazil,
Czech Republic, Great Britain,
Iceland, Peru, Russia,
United States

COLORS

Green

PRIMARY USES

Assists with grounding and centering, promotes prosperity and abundance, aids in manifestation, enhances intuition, promotes psychic abilities, helps improve gardening abilities

CHAKRA

Heart

PLACEMENT

Place on or touching the heart chakra, place in the garden or in a garden shed, place in the home's prosperity corner, keep in meditation area, carry in a pocket

ORANGE

Calcite

Orange calcite in its rough form has a chalky/waxy surface with a slight luster. It is light orange with white striations. When tumbled and polished, it loses its waxy appearance and has a high luster.

ORIGIN

Belgium, Brazil, Czech Republic, Great Britain, Iceland, Peru, Russia, United States

COLORS

Orange

PRIMARY USES

Facilitates integration of spiritual and physical, enhances self-esteem, boosts creativity, increases positive energy, promotes healthy sexuality, improves all types of energy

CHAKRA

Sacral, solar plexus

PLACEMENT

Place on or touching the appropriate chakras, keep in areas of creativity, hold in the receiving (nondominant) hand, carry in pants pocket

PINK (MANGANO CALCITE)

Calcite

Light pink to peach in color, mangano calcite is also known as pink calcite. The stone is opaque with a waxy finish in the rough state and a smooth, shiny finish for the tumbled stones. It has white striations and bands throughout.

ORIGIN

Belgium, Brazil,
Czech Republic, Great Britain,
Iceland, Peru, Russia,
United States

COLORS

Peachy pink to pink

PRIMARY USES

Amplifies Reiki energy and other healing energies, assists contact with higher entities, promotes love of all, increases an awareness of being one with all, opens the heart

CHAKRA

Heart

PLACEMENT

Place on or touching the heart chakra, hold in either hand depending on use (giving, or dominant, for Reiki energy or sharing love; receiving, or non-dominant, for universal love), carry in a shirt pocket, wear around the neck as a pendant, keep in meditation area, keep in any healing space such as a sickroom

WHITE

Calcite

White calcite in its rough form can look like conventional boxy crystals, like slices or leaves of white stone, or even white bubbles. It appears to be lit by an inner glow.

ORIGIN

Belgium, Brazil, Czech Republic, Great Britain, Iceland, Peru, Russia, United States

COLORS

White

PRIMARY USES

Facilitates communication with higher realms in connection with the crown chakra, cleanses energetic fields, amplifies energy

CHAKRA

Crown

PLACEMENT

Place on or touching any or all chakras for cleansing, carry in a pocket, hold in either hand, keep in meditation space, place under the pillow to facilitate dream connection with higher realms

YELLOW

Calcite

This crystal is often a pretty lemon yellow, causing some people to refer to it as lemon calcite. It may also be the color of honey. Polished stones are clear.

ORIGIN

Belgium, Brazil,
Czech Republic, Great Britain,
Iceland, Peru, Russia,
United States

COLORS

Yellow

PRIMARY USES

Increases self-worth and self-confidence, promotes joy, enhances optimism, encourages empathy

CHAKRA

Solar plexus

PLACEMENT

Place on or touching the solar plexus chakra, hold in the receiving (nondominant) hand, wear as jewelry of any kind, carry in a pocket

Carnelian

This stone ranges in color from orange to orange-red, and it may have inclusions or bands of brown, yellow, or white. One form, spiderweb carnelian, has multiple threadlike bands of white running through it. Carnelian is a translucent, vividly colored stone.

ORIGIN

Czech Republic, Great Britain, Iceland, India, Peru, Romania

COLORS

Orange, brownish orange, red-orange

PRIMARY USES

Promotes security and safety, promotes courage, amplifies or provides energy, promotes willpower and determination, aids in overcoming abuse, increases vitality

CHAKRA

Root, sacral

PLACEMENT

Place on or touching the appropriate chakras, carry in pants pocket, wear around the waist in a pouch, place next to the bed to promote sexual energy, keep in the refrigerator or food cupboards to promote willpower

Celestite

A translucent blue with multiple facets, celestite is an incredibly beautiful crystal. The color can range from the lightest to the deepest of blues, with tinges of gray, green, or violet within. Some celestite is also yellow or white, but blue is most common. It is a high-vibration stone.

ORIGIN

Egypt, Great Britain, Madagascar, Mexico, Peru

COLORS

Blue, white, yellow

PRIMARY USES

Facilitates communication with higher beings, provides insight and intuition, supports communication with the Divine, assists with spiritual development, aids in achieving enlightenment, promotes creativity, promotes inner peace, uplifts the spirit

CHAKRA

Third eye, crown

PLACEMENT

Place on or touching the appropriate chakras, wear as necklace or earrings, hold in hands during meditation, keep in meditation area, place on desk or in creative area

BLUE

Chalcedony

Blue is one of the colors of chalcedony, a silica crystal made up of morganite and quartz. It has a soft, almost ethereal, blue color and a lustrous surface. It is a relatively hard crystal and makes beautiful jewelry.

ORIGIN

Austria, Brazil, Czech Republic, Great Britain, Iceland, Mexico, Morocco, Russia, Turkey, United States

COLORS

Light to medium blue

PRIMARY USES

Promotes good dreams, creates balance in all aspects of self, reduces negative emotions, increases intuition, improves communication

CHAKRA

Third eye, throat

PLACEMENT

Place on or touching the appropriate chakras, hold in your receiving (nondominant) hand, wear as jewelry (particularly around the neck or earrings), keep in a room that needs calm or facilitated communication, carry in a pocket, place under the pillow or mattress or on the bedside table to promote good dreams, keep in meditation area

Chrysoberyl

Alexandrite (see page 249) is one form of chrysoberyl. The most common forms are translucent irregular rocks in shades of yellow and green. It is a very hard stone, so it holds up well when used with other stones or carried in the pocket.

ORIGIN

Brazil, Russia, Sri Lanka, Tanzania, United States

COLORS

Green or yellowish green

PRIMARY USES

Promotes personal drive, facilitates goal setting, establishes self-identity, promotes self-esteem

CHAKRA

Solar plexus

PLACEMENT

Place on or touching the solar plexus chakra, hold in either hand, wear as a bracelet or ring, carry in a pocket

Chrysoprase

A variety of chalcedony, chrysoprase comes in a variety of green shades. The stone is opaque and may have banding of white, brown, or black. Chrysoprase may also be called prase.

ORIGIN

Australia, Brazil, Poland, Russia, Tanzania, United States

COLORS

Apple green to deep green

PRIMARY USES

Opens the heart, facilitates love, draws prosperity, facilitates compassion, imparts hope, fights despair

CHAKRA

Heart

PLACEMENT

Place on or touching the heart chakra, hold in either hand, carry in a pocket, keep in a cashbox or wallet, keep in the prosperity corner of the home or any room

Cinnabar

This bright red mineral may have a dull or a lustrous appearance. It is made from mercury sulfide and may also be called vermillion. It may have mineral inclusions with a gold color and nonmetallic luster. It is known as the merchant's stone.

ORIGIN

China, United States

COLORS

Brick red, sometimes with gray or gold

PRIMARY USES

Supports manifestation, promotes success in business, attracts abundance, increases persuasive powers, increases personal power, promotes personal transformation

CHAKRA

Root, sacral

PLACEMENT

Place on or touching the appropriate chakras, hold in the receiving (nondominant) hand, keep in cashbox or safe, place on work desk, keep in wallet, carry in pants pocket, bring to sales calls

Citrine

This yellow crystal may come in clusters and geodes, or it may come in individual points or polished stones. Naturally occurring citrine is yellow and translucent. Some people also create a citrine-like stone by heat-treating amethyst until it turns yellow. Heat-treated amethyst/citrine tends to have a more vivid yellow color. It may share the same metaphysical properties as naturally occurring citrine, although they may be slightly less or not as consistent. Many people prefer working only with the natural stone because its energy is consistent.

ORIGIN

Brazil, France, Great Britain, Madagascar, Peru, Russia, United States

COLORS

Yellow

PRIMARY USES

Fosters self-esteem, promotes prosperity and abundance, enhances creativity, transforms negative energy to positive, encourages generosity, protects against self-destructive tendencies

CHAKRA

Solar plexus

PLACEMENT

Place on or touching the solar plexus chakra, wear as jewelry (particularly bracelet or ring), hold in the receiving (nondominant) hand, carry in a pocket, keep in wallet or cashbox, keep in the prosperity corner of the home, place on a desk or in areas requiring creative thought

Danburite

This clear stone comes in many colors, with banding in white or gray. It is a high-vibration crystal. It is a relatively hard stone, and it may come polished, in clusters, or in points. All danburite basically has the same energetic qualities, although you can use different colors with the specific chakras those colors correspond to: yellow (solar plexus), white (crown), pink (crown), light purple (third eye).

ORIGIN

Japan, Mexico, Russia, Switzerland, United States

COLOR

Yellow, white, pink, light purple

PRIMARY USES

Promotes unconditional love, supports intuition, enhances higher communication, assists with aura purification, aids in communication with higher self or the Divine, aids enlightenment

CHAKRA

Heart, throat, third eye, crown

PLACEMENT

Place on or touching the appropriate chakras, wear as jewelry (around the neck or as earrings), carry in a pocket, keep in meditation area

(GYPSUM)

Desert Rose

This unique crystal is so named because of its resemblance to a rose. It is a gypsum stone in the colors of sand, with bands of white across the top of each "petal." The formation is unique, as the stone is rounded with multilayered petals. It's also known as a selenite rose. Be careful with gypsum because it is soft and brittle. Don't use water or salt to cleanse this crystal.

ORIGIN

Austria, France, Germany, Great Britain, Greece, Poland, Russia, United States

COLORS

Sand-colored with white

PRIMARY USES

Facilitates communication with higher self and the Divine, focuses the mind, promotes acceptance, provides calming, offers spiritual comfort, aids in cleansing energy

CHAKRA

Third eye, crown

PLACEMENT

Place on or touching the appropriate chakras, hold gently in either hand, keep in meditation area

Diamond

Rough diamonds look very different from their jewelry counterparts because they have not been cut or polished. Rough diamonds are translucent, and they may be found in many colors, such as white, black, gray, or yellow. They tend to be very small and expensive. All diamonds, regardless of color, are essentially used in the same way. Colored diamonds sold as jewelry are often treated or enhanced in some manner.

ORIGIN

Angola, Australia, Botswana, Brazil, India, Russia, South Africa, United States

COLORS

Gray, black, clear, white, yellow, brown, pink, blue

PRIMARY USES

Provides purification and cleansing, supports abundance, amplifies energy, aids connection to higher self, heals the aura

CHAKRA

Crown

PLACEMENT

Directly touching the crown chakra, wear as necklace or earrings, carry in a pocket, place anywhere in need of purification or cleansing, keep in a cash box or wallet, keep in meditation area

Dioptase

A beautiful deep green stone, dioptase typically appears in small clusters or as small individual points. This stone is fairly rare, so it is an expensive one.

ORIGIN

Chile, Congo, Iran, North Africa, Peru, Russia

COLORS

Emerald green to deep blue-green

PRIMARY USES

Supports love, heals the heart, helps with present-time focus, promotes prosperity and abundance

CHAKRA

Heart

PLACEMENT

Place on or touching the heart chakra, hold in the receiving (nondominant) hand, keep in a wallet or cashbox, place in a room to facilitate relationships and love, carry in a pocket, wear as jewelry to stimulate focus on the now

Emerald

A bright green precious gemstone, emeralds are transparent and translucent. In their rough form, the crystal is cloudy, but once cut, it is brilliantly clear and beautiful.

ORIGIN

Austria, Brazil, Egypt, India, Tanzania, Zimbabwe

COLORS

Green

PRIMARY USES

Supports success in love, promotes faithfulness, creates unity in partnerships and relationships, increases positivity while releasing negativity, imparts wisdom

CHAKRA

Heart

PLACEMENT

Place on or touching the heart chakra, wear in jewelry (particularly necklace, bracelet, or ring), use in an engagement ring to strengthen the partnership, carry in a pocket

Epidote

Epidote is made up of lustrous, often elongated crystals. Colors range from yellowish green to very dark green. When faceted and polished, the stone is exceptionally clear.

ORIGIN

Austria, Canada, Egypt, France, Germany, Greenland, Japan, Norway, Russia, Sweden, United States

COLORS

Yellow-green to green

PRIMARY USES

Promotes abundance and prosperity, improves relationships, promotes attunement to spirit, assists in letting go, serves as a catalyst for change

CHAKRA

Heart

PLACEMENT

Place on or touching the heart chakra, keep in the prosperity corner of the home or room, keep in meditation area

BLUE

Fluorite

Fluorite is a relatively soft mineral that comes in a variety of colors. Blue fluorite can come in a range of blue to blue-green and is exceptionally clear. This translucent stone scratches easily, and the scratches show up very well. Use care when carrying it in a pocket or using it with other stones. Don't use water or salt to cleanse this crystal.

ORIGIN

Australia, Brazil, China, Germany, Great Britain, Mexico, Peru, United States

COLORS

Blue

PRIMARY USES

Calms, creates rational thought, soothes mental or emotional chaos, facilitates communication, improves insight, facilitates kind honesty, supports spiritual awakening

CHAKRA

Third eye, throat

PLACEMENT

Place on or touching the appropriate chakras, wear as jewelry (particularly necklace and earrings), hold in your receiving (nondominant) hand, keep in a room that requires a sense of calm, keep anywhere enhanced communication is needed such as a classroom or boardroom, keep in meditation area

GREEN

Fluorite

This crystal may range from light aqua to dark green. It is a very clear crystal that is also quite soft. Therefore, it's important to protect it from scratching, so exercise caution if you carry it in your pocket or use it with other crystals. Don't use water or salt to cleanse this crystal.

ORIGIN

Australia, Brazil, China, Germany, Great Britain, Mexico, Peru, United States

COLORS

Green

PRIMARY USES

Provides energy, detoxifies and cleanses chakras, assists with healing from heart-break, improves focus, helps prevent effects of electromagnetic energy

CHAKRA

Heart

PLACEMENT

Place on or touching the heart chakra, wear as jewelry (particularly a necklace), hold in either hand, place in an area with heavy electromagnetic or electrical energy (such as near a computer or television)

Fluorite

A light to dark purple or violet gemstone of exceptional clarity, purple fluorite is a high-vibration stone. It typically has a smooth surface, because it is at its most beautiful tumbled and polished. Beware of scratching this soft gemstone, and use care when working with other crystals or carrying it in a pocket. Don't use water or salt to cleanse this crystal.

ORIGIN

Australia, Brazil, China, Germany, Great Britain, Mexico, Peru, United States

COLORS

Light purple to violet

PRIMARY USES

Facilitates connection with higher self, heightens psychic abilities and intuition, fosters peace and calmness, sharpens mental ability and enhances focus, aids in decision-making

CHAKRA

Third eye, crown

PLACEMENT

Place on or touching the appropriate chakras, wear as a necklace or earrings, hold in the receiving (nondominant) hand, keep in meditation space, place in a work area to enhance focus

RAINBOW
Fluorite

Arguably one of the most beautiful and interesting crystals, rainbow fluorite carries bands of clear color throughout each crystal. Common band colors in rainbow fluorite include blue, violet, purple, green, aqua, and pink. Cleanse and charge rainbow fluorite after every use to keep its clear vibrational energy pure. Protect from scratching. Don't use water or salt to cleanse this crystal.

ORIGIN

Australia, Brazil, China, Germany, Great Britain, Mexico, Peru, United States

COLORS

Multicolored

PRIMARY USES

Balances chakras (as well as body, mind, and spirit), harmonizes emotions, facilitates communication with higher self and higher beings including the Divine, promotes intuition and inspiration, aids spiritual awakening and enlightenment

CHAKRA

Solar plexus, heart, throat, third eye, crown

PLACEMENT

Place on or touching the appropriate chakras, wear as jewelry, keep close to the heart, hold in the receiving (nondominant) hand, keep in meditation space, place in an area where a boost in creativity is needed

Fuchsite

Also known as chrome mica, fuchsite is a green, rough stone with a sparkle to it when the mica catches the light. When polished, it ranges from light to deep green, and it often occurs with bits of ruby in it (see Ruby in Fuchsite on page 321). It is commonly known as a healer's stone.

ORIGIN

Brazil, India, Russia

COLORS

Light to very dark green

PRIMARY USES

Provides intuitive information to healers, resolves power struggles, promotes understanding in relationship difficulties, imparts self-worth, clears heart chakra blockages

CHAKRA

Heart

PLACEMENT

Place on or touching the heart chakra, hold in the receiving (nondominant) hand for medical intuition, carry in a pocket, wear as jewelry, keep in a healer's space, keep in meditation space, place in a sickroom next to the bed or under the mattress or pillow

Garnet

Garnets can come in an array of colors, although the most commonly sought-after garnets are red. Red garnets help with issues of safety, security, and passion. Green garnets strengthen unconditional love and promote prosperity. Yellow and gold garnets bolster self-esteem. Orange garnets strengthen sense of identity within a group. This semi-precious gemstone is transparent and translucent and characterized by deeply vivid colors.

ORIGIN

All over the world

COLORS

Red, orange, yellow, brown, green, gold

PRIMARY USES

Aids chakra cleansing, supports grounding, enhances passion and love, promotes helping one another, cleanses negative energies, amplifies other crystals

CHAKRA

Root (red), heart (green), solar plexus (yellow or gold), sacral (orange)

PLACEMENT

Place on or touching any or all chakras for chakra cleansing (with other crystals for amplification), hold in either hand, wear as jewelry, keep in meditation area

Hematite

Hematite is a deep red to silver lustrous crystal that has a metallic sheen when polished. Hematite is made of iron oxide. Its root, *hemo*, comes from the Greek word for blood and refers to the red color. Many people believe hematite is magnetic, but this is true only of artificially magnetized hematite. Stick with natural hematite.

ORIGIN

Brazil, Canada, Great Britain, Sweden, Switzerland

COLORS

Silver, red

PRIMARY USES

Absorbs negative energy, aids grounding, calms stress, helps to develop self-control, provides equilibrium and balance, detoxifies

CHAKRA

Root

PLACEMENT

Place on or touching the root chakra, wear as a ring, carry in pants pocket, place in any area to transform negative energy

Herkimer Diamond

A Herkimer diamond is a double-terminated clear quartz point (points at both ends). The crystal is clear, although it may have a few inclusions. It is a very high-vibration stone.

ORIGIN

Mexico, Spain, Tanzania, United States

COLORS

Clear

PRIMARY USES

Amplifies energy (both one's own and from other crystals), detoxifies, cleanses the aura and chakras, facilitates connection with the Divine, aids in achieving enlightenment and moving the spirit to a higher plane, boosts psychic abilities

CHAKRA

Crown

PLACEMENT

Place on or touching the crown chakra, place on all other chakras along with other chakra stones, wear as jewelry (particularly necklace or earrings), hold in the receiving (nondominant) hand, keep in meditation area

Howlite

You'll often find this white stone with black bands dyed a vivid turquoise blue. It is then used in jewelry as an inexpensive replacement for turquoise or lapis lazuli, because when it is dyed it has a similar appearance. If you're looking for the properties of turquoise (see page 340) or lapis lazuli (see page 302), then make sure you're not looking at dyed howlite, as the properties differ between the stones.

ORIGIN

United States

COLORS

White

PRIMARY USES

Balances chakras, connects with higher consciousness, calms and soothes, treats insomnia, teaches patience

CHAKRA

Crown

PLACEMENT

Place on or touching the crown chakra, hold in either hand, place under a pillow or on a bedside table, keep in meditation area

Iolite

Iolite—also known as *water sapphire*—is a lovely indigo or violet clear stone. It often has a tinge of gray in it as well. It gets its name from the Greek word *ion,* meaning violet. It is a moderately hard stone, but it is best to keep it protected when it is used with other stones.

ORIGIN

United States

COLORS

Indigo to violet

PRIMARY USES

Amplifies or encourages psychic insight, eases addiction, increases focus, tunes in to guidance from your higher self or higher beings, sparks inspiration

CHAKRA

Third eye, crown

PLACEMENT

Place on the appropriate chakras, wear as jewelry (particularly earrings), carry in a pocket, keep in meditation area, hold in the receiving (nondominant) hand

Iron Pyrite

Iron pyrite is known as fool's gold for a good reason: it looks a lot like gold but doesn't have the same value as the precious metal. You may find it as gold flecks within a darker stone, or you may find full nuggets or cut shapes of iron pyrite. It is opaque with a shiny golden luster.

ORIGIN

Canada, Chile, Great Britain, Peru, United States

COLORS

Gold

PRIMARY USES

Promotes success in business, aids in establishing prosperity, brings good fortune, strengthens willpower

CHAKRA

Solar plexus

PLACEMENT

Place on solar plexus chakra, carry in a pocket, keep in the prosperity corner of house or room, place in a safe or cashbox, keep on work desk for business success

Jade

The most common color of jade is watery green, but jade comes in many other colors, including white, purple, red, and black. Green jade helps improve relationships via the heart chakra. White jade aids focus and decision-making. Purple jade facilitates the discovery of inner peace. Jade is smooth with a translucent, creamy quality. It is a very popular semiprecious gemstone used in jewelry and carvings. Don't use water or salt to cleanse this crystal.

ORIGIN

China, Italy, Middle East, Russia, United States

COLORS

Green, white, purple, red, black, orange

PRIMARY USES

Affords good luck, imparts peace, helps with self-definition and self-knowledge, improves insight and guidance

CHAKRA

All chakras, depending on color

PLACEMENT

Place on or touching the appropriate chakras, wear as jewelry, carry in a pocket, hold in either hand, keep in meditation space

Jasper

Jasper comes in many colors. All are opaque with bands or spots running throughout. It often has interesting natural designs, which you'll see in the polished stones or slabs. While the uses below apply to all jasper crystals, green jasper tends to create harmony in relationships, red enhances vibrancy and passion, and yellow strengthens perseverance.

ORIGIN

All over the world

COLORS

Brown, white, red, green, yellow, blue, black

PRIMARY USES

Provides stability, improves grounding

CHAKRA

All chakras, depending on color

PLACEMENT

Place on or touching the appropriate chakras, place anywhere on the body where healing is needed, carry in a pocket, hold in either hand, wear as jewelry

Jet

Jet looks like an opaque, dark black rock. It may be tumbled smooth, polished, or in its rough form. It has a dark, waxy but dull luster. It may also be called black amber, although it isn't a form of amber. Instead, it is fossilized wood that, over time, has turned into lignite coal.

ORIGIN

All over the world

COLORS

Black

PRIMARY USES

Provides protection, aids in grounding, absorbs negative energy, helps with mourning, purifies

CHAKRA

Root

PLACEMENT

Place on or touching the root chakra, carry in pants pocket, hold in either hand, keep in a room to dispel negative energy, bring to a funeral

Kunzite

Kunzite is a very high-vibration stone. It is lightly colored, typically pink, and the stones are exceptionally clear. Rough stones may have some striations in them.

ORIGIN

Afghanistan, Brazil, United States

COLORS

Pink, clear, light purple

PRIMARY USES

Enhances communication with the Divine or higher entities, allows for a full experience of emotions, provides emotional support for women, provides peace and calmness

CHAKRA

Heart, crown

PLACEMENT

Place on or touching the appropriate chakras, hold in either hand, wear as jewelry (particularly necklace or earrings), keep in meditation area, place in any room for peaceful confrontation

Kyanite

Blue kyanite is a silicate mineral and is one of several colors of kyanite. It ranges in hue from a soft gray blue to a deeper blue with bands of white or gray running through it. In its rough form, kyanite looks like a long slab with blades. When polished, it is smooth with a soft luster. The stone may be transparent or it may be opaque. You may also find blades of kyanite embedded in larger pieces of stone. Don't use water or salt to cleanse this crystal.

ORIGIN

Brazil

COLORS

Blue

PRIMARY USES

Inspires fairness, promotes loyalty, improves communication, fosters truth-telling, enhances self-expression, fights self-destructive behaviors, aids with memory

CHAKRA

Third eye, throat

PLACEMENT

Place on or touching the appropriate chakras, wear as jewelry (particularly necklace or earrings), carry in a shirt pocket, wear around the neck to enhance communication and self-expression, keep anywhere enhanced communication is needed (such as a classroom or boardroom), tape to the bottom of a work or study chair to support focus and memory

GREEN

Kyanite

Green kyanite is a silicate mineral with white or gray running through it. In its rough form, kyanite appears as a long slab with blades. When polished, it is smooth with a soft luster and swirling bands of white or gray. The stone may be transparent or opaque. You may also find blades of green kyanite embedded in larger pieces of stone. Don't use water or salt to cleanse this crystal.

ORIGIN

Brazil

COLORS

Green

PRIMARY USES

Releases negative energy, balances the heart chakra, aligns all chakras, facilitates comprehension of information from higher sources, allows for the discernment of other people's motivations

CHAKRA

Heart, third eye

PLACEMENT

Place on or touching the appropriate chakras, wear as jewelry (particularly necklace or earrings), carry in a pocket near the heart, place in any space that needs energizing or cleansing

Labradorite

Labradorite's beauty comes from its mysterious swirling colors and lustrous appearance. Labradorite can range from milky clear to a clear gray, with flashes of blue, purple, green, and other swirling colors that show up when it catches the light. It is a high-vibration stone.

ORIGIN

Canada, Italy, Scandinavia

COLORS

Clear or dark with flashes of blue, gold, purple, and green

PRIMARY USES

Enhances communication with the Divine or higher beings, helps tune in to psychic energy and intuition, balances mind and spirit, protects against negative energy, provides discernment, cleanses and heals the aura

CHAKRA

Third eye, crown

PLACEMENT

Place on or touching the appropriate chakras, place directly on the body as needed for healing, wear as jewelry (particularly earrings and necklace), hold in either hand, keep in meditation area, place under the pillow for insightful dreams

Lapis Lazuli

This rich blue stone is opaque with veins of gold or white running through it. In the middle ages, lapis was ground and used as ultramarine, a pigment for oil paints. Some manufacturers dye howlite (see page 292) to look like this stone, so it is important to make sure you are using genuine lapis lazuli.

ORIGIN

Chile, Egypt, Italy, Middle East, United States

COLORS

Deep blue with gold flecks

PRIMARY USES

Enhances communication, increases truth and integrity, opens the third eye, allows for speaking one's truth, connects to spiritual and higher wisdom

CHAKRA

Throat, third eye

PLACEMENT

Place on or touching the appropriate chakras, wear as jewelry (particularly necklace and earrings), carry in a pocket, keep in a room where communication is essential, hold in either hand, keep in meditation area

Lepidolite

Lepidolite has a pretty pink, lilac, or purple color with striations of brown or white in it. It is opaque but with luster. You can find it in polished stones or in natural (rough) stones.

ORIGIN

Brazil, Czech Republic, Dominican Republic, United States

COLORS

Pink, lilac

PRIMARY USES

Relieves stress, promotes calmness, improves meditation, awakens insight, facilitates connection with the Divine

CHAKRA

Third eye, crown

PLACEMENT

Place on or touching the appropriate chakras, wear as jewelry (necklace or earrings), carry in a pocket, hold in either hand, keep in meditation area

Lodestone

Lodestone—also known as *magnetite*—is black iron oxide that is naturally magnetic. As a result, lodestone often has small pieces of magnetic materials sticking to it, making it appear a little bit fuzzy, as if in need of a good shave. Keep it in a plastic container to keep the small bits of iron sticking to the lodestone. It is a very heavy stone for its size.

ORIGIN

Austria, Central America, Finland, India, Italy, North America

COLORS

Black

PRIMARY USES

Promotes grounding, aligns chakras, magnifies the Law of Attraction

CHAKRA

Root

PLACEMENT

Place on or near the root chakra, carry in pants pockets, hold in hands for grounding

Malachite

A beautiful deep green stone, malachite is opaque with swirls of lighter green or white throughout. In its tumbled form, the striations form interesting designs similar to those found in marble. Malachite has a little bit of sheen to it and polishes to a high gloss. It is the stone of protection for airline workers.

ORIGIN

Congo, Middle East, Romania, Russia, Zambia

COLORS

Green

PRIMARY USES

Provides spiritual and energetic protection, offers protection for airline workers and travelers, overcomes phobias, encourages risk-taking, helps share one's truth with others, boosts mood (particularly in the case of depression)

CHAKRA

Heart

PLACEMENT

Place on or touching the heart chakra, wear in jewelry (bracelets and rings), hold in either hand, carry in a pocket or place in carry-on luggage when flying

Moldavite

Moldavite is a substance with a science fiction–worthy origin story. It is believed it forms as the result of a meteor impact. This "outer space" crystal has a deep olive green color with a bumpy texture and a lustrous sheen.

ORIGIN

Czech Republic, Germany, Moldova

COLORS

Olive, bottle green

PRIMARY USES

Eases negative thinking about finances, helps in the discovery of one's life's purpose, helps deepen meditation and insight, fosters self-love, assists in living with honor and integrity

CHAKRA

Heart, third eye, crown

PLACEMENT

Place on or touching the appropriate chakras, hold in the receiving (nondominant) hand, keep in meditation space, keep in wallet or cash box, wear as a pendant around the neck

Moonstone

Moonstone looks like the moon reflected. It is typically peach, white, or black with swirling colors inside, depending on the light. All the colors share the same basic energetic qualities. Milky white moonstone is the most common color. It gets its shimmer from a property of gemstones known as adularescence, which is also found in labradorite.

ORIGIN

Australia, Brazil, India, Sri Lanka

COLORS

White, cream, black, peach

PRIMARY USES

Assists communication with higher self or the Divine, aids connection with spiritual beings, increases psychic abilities, supports wish fulfillment

CHAKRA

Third eye, crown

PLACEMENT

Place on or touching the appropriate chakras, hold in either hand, place under a pillow, keep in meditation area, wear as jewelry (particularly necklace and earrings)

Muscovite

Muscovite is a form of mica, with interesting formations that look like flakes or slabs coming from the main stone. It has a pearlescent, multicolor luster. The same energetic qualities are common to all colors of muscovite crystals. Muscovite is very brittle, so use and store it carefully. Don't use water or salt to cleanse this crystal.

ORIGIN

Austria, Brazil, Czech Republic, Russia, Switzerland, United States

COLORS

Gray, green, pink/red, gold

PRIMARY USES

Enhances connection with the Divine or spiritual beings, connects with one's higher self, provides guidance and insight, promotes intuition

CHAKRA

Third eye, crown

PLACEMENT

Place on or touching the appropriate chakras, hold gently in either hand, keep in meditation space, place next to the bed for guidance while dreaming

Obsidian

Made from volcanic glass, obsidian is a lustrous stone that may be smooth or have rough, craggy edges. The most common color is black, but you can find it in other colors as well, noted below. Obsidian is also the stone that makes up Apache tears (see page 255).

ORIGIN

All around the world

COLORS

Black, black with white, green, blue, red

PRIMARY USES

Supports grounding, clears root chakra blockages, absorbs negative energy, calms grief, provides strength and energy, exposes negative emotions, provides spiritual and emotional protection

CHAKRA

Root (black), heart (green)

PLACEMENT

Place on or touching the appropriate chakras, hold in either hand, carry in pants pocket, place in any room to absorb negative emotions, keep in meditation space

Obsidian

This form of obsidian is black to greenish black and has white splotches on it that resemble snowflakes. It is an opaque stone, and it can either be rough or tumbled and polished to a slight sheen.

ORIGIN

All around the world

COLORS

Black to greenish black

PRIMARY USES

Increases feelings of safety and security, calms, provides spiritual protection, helps eliminate disruptive thoughts and beliefs

CHAKRA

Root

PLACEMENT

Place on or touching the root chakra, hold in either hand, carry in pants pocket

Onyx

Onyx comes in many colors, although you mostly find it in black, black with white bands, or white with black bands. All the colors have the same metaphysical properties. It is a smooth, dark, heavy stone that is a form of chalcedony.

ORIGIN

Brazil, Italy, Mexico, Russia, South Africa, United States

COLORS

Black, white, gray, red, yellow, brown, blue

PRIMARY USES

Provides strength, promotes grounding and centering, promotes stamina, absorbs negative energy, protects spiritually

CHAKRA

Root

PLACEMENT

Place on or touching the root chakra, wear as jewelry (particularly bracelets and rings), hold in either hand, carry in pants pocket, place in any room to absorb negative energy and provide protection, keep in meditation space

Opal

Opals are cloudy, soft, luminous gemstones that offer brilliant flashes of color. Opals come in an array of colors, including white, black, and blue. This is a high-vibration stone. This gemstone is very soft and can damage easily, so use caution when wearing it, cleaning it, or using it with other stones. Don't use water or salt to cleanse this crystal.

ORIGIN

Australia, Canada, Great Britain, Honduras, Mexico, Peru

COLORS

White, black, blue, pink, red, orange, yellow, green

PRIMARY USES

Provides inspiration, sparks creativity, assists in communication with higher beings or the Divine, aids communication with higher self, promotes spontaneity, and helps connect to others through unconditional love

CHAKRA

All chakras, depending on color, especially the crown

PLACEMENT

Place on or touching any chakra (especially the crown chakra), hold in the receiving (non-dominant) hand, wear as any type of jewelry, keep in meditation area, place in creative workspaces

Peridot

This gemstone is clear and comes in greens ranging from light olive green to bright apple green. It may have small black or brown flecks within the crystal. It is often cut and polished into faceted gemstones for jewelry.

ORIGIN

Brazil, Canary Islands, Egypt, Ireland, Russia, Sri Lanka

COLORS

Green

PRIMARY USES

Opens the heart chakra, promotes love, eases emotional trauma, promotes understanding of relationships, protects the aura, cleanses the body's energetic system (chakras, aura, meridians)

CHAKRA

Heart, solar plexus

PLACEMENT

Place on or touching the appropriate chakras, wear as jewelry of any kind, carry in a pocket, hold in the receiving (nondominant) hand, keep in meditation area, carry close when working on relationships

Prehnite

A slightly transparent green gemstone, prehnite is muddy green or olive green. It has small striations throughout, and the surface of the rough stone is bumpy. When polished, the stone is luminous and fairly transparent. It is a high-vibration stone, often referred to as the stone of prophecy.

ORIGIN

South Africa

COLORS

Green

PRIMARY USES

Assists with shamanic work, enhances psychic energy (particularly precognition), facilitates connection with the Divine or higher entities, helps build trust in the Divine, cleanses and detoxifies energy fields

CHAKRA

Heart

PLACEMENT

Place on or touching the heart chakra, wear as jewelry (necklace and earrings), keep in meditation area and healing area (if performing healing work), hold in either hand for healing work, carry in a pocket for shamanic work

CLEAR

Quartz

This clear stone is transparent and translucent. It comes in clusters, geodes, points, double terminated points (known as Herkimer diamonds), and polished or rough stones. It is a high-vibration stone and is known as the master healer because it works with all conditions.

ORIGIN

All over the world

COLORS

Clear or milky white

PRIMARY USES

Amplifies energies, cleanses spaces, works as a master healer to help with any type of healing, increases energy, cleanses and charges crystals, provides protection

CHAKRA

All chakras, but particularly the crown

PLACEMENT

Place on or touching any chakra or specifically the crown chakra, use in grids, use with other stones for amplification, place anywhere on the body healing is needed, carry in a pocket, keep in a room or place where protection or cleansing is needed, wear as jewelry

ROSE

Quartz

This quartz is partially transparent with a milky pink color. You may find it in points or polished stones, and it is often carved into interesting shapes for jewelry. Rose quartz is known as the stone of love and is often used for all types of issues associated with love.

ORIGIN

Brazil, India, Japan, Madagascar, South Africa, United States

COLORS

Pink

PRIMARY USES

Promotes and strengthens all types of love, fosters unconditional love, promotes joy, promotes emotional healing, fosters faith, strengthens hope, helps overcome despair, instills calm and peacefulness

CHAKRA

Root, heart

PLACEMENT

Place on or touching the appropriate chakras, wear as any type of jewelry, carry in a pocket, hold in both hands, place all around the house to promote a loving family atmosphere

RUTILATED

Quartz

Rutilated (or rutile) quartz is clear to smoky or golden, with long brown, reddish, or black strands running through it. Rutilated means the stone contains fine needles of titanium dioxide. You can find rutilated quartz in any form that you'd normally find quartz, such as clusters, points, and polished stones.

ORIGIN

All around the world

COLORS

Clear to golden, with black, reddish, or brown strands

PRIMARY USES

Provides energy (spiritual, emotional, and physical), improves focus and concentration, helps clarify one's life's path, increases connection with higher self, banishes negative energy, facilitates emotional release, amplifies energy

CHAKRA

Solar plexus, crown

PLACEMENT

Place on or touching the appropriate chakras, keep in a desk drawer to enhance focus or concentration, hold in either hand, carry in a pocket, keep in meditation area

Quartz

A member of the quartz family, smoky quartz has a beautiful brown to gray smoke color. It occurs naturally in the Earth, but it can also be simulated in a laboratory, so it's important to check the origins of the specimen. It is a clear stone when polished, and mostly clear to slightly opaque when in its rough form.

ORIGIN

All around the world

COLORS

Gray to brownish gray

PRIMARY USES

Absorbs negative energy and increases positive energy, promotes grounding, increases vibrational energy, detoxifies, aids in letting go of past hurt

CHAKRA

Root, crown

PLACEMENT

Place on or touching the appropriate chakras, carry in a pocket, wear as jewelry, hold in either hand, keep in meditation space, sprinkle around any area (such as the perimeter of the home) to block negative energy and increase positive energy

Rhodochrosite

A pretty pink stone, rhodochrosite has bands of white or black throughout. It is a partially translucent stone. This is quite a soft stone, so use caution when working with other stones. Don't use water or salt to cleanse this crystal. Color variations arise from impurities.

ORIGIN

Argentina, Russia, South Africa, United States, Uruguay

COLORS

Pink to orange-pink

PRIMARY USES

Promotes unconditional love, helps heal a broken heart and deep emotional issues, attracts love, heals issues of self-worth, alleviates past hurts

CHAKRA

Root, heart

PLACEMENT

Place on or touching the appropriate chakras, carry in pants pocket, place anywhere on the body emotional pain manifests physically

Ruby

Rubies are pink to red and appear opaque, but when polished and cut become a vivid, transparent red. These precious gemstones are used in jewelry, but the rough stones also offer powerful healing properties.

ORIGIN

Cambodia, India, Kenya, Madagascar, Mexico, Russia, Sri Lanka

COLORS

Red

PRIMARY USES

Promotes vitality, strengthens passion and drive (sexual and otherwise), energizes, promotes love, enhances joy of life

CHAKRA

Root, heart

PLACEMENT

Place on or touching the appropriate chakras, wear as any type of jewelry, place under a pillow or mattress for revitalizing sexual energy, carry in a pocket to reenergize

Ruby in Fuchsite

Ruby occurs naturally in fuchsite. The fuchsite has light to deep green coloring that appears almost creamy, and when it has ruby in it, the fuchsite contains spots that vary in size and are pink to deep red.

ORIGIN

Brazil, India, Russia

COLORS

Green with pink or red

PRIMARY USES

Opens the heart chakra, promotes love, fosters strength and willpower, increases intellect, sharpens focus, provides protection of spiritual, emotional, and mental energy

CHAKRA

Root, heart

PLACEMENT

Place on or touching the appropriate chakras, wear as any type of jewelry, carry in a pocket, hold in either hand

Sapphire

Sapphire is a form of the mineral corundum (which is also the mineral of rubies). It is very hard and durable. Sapphire comes in many colors, although the most commonly recognized is the blue sapphire. While stones of different colors share many qualities, there are some differences among them. Blue sapphire opens the third eye and aids connection with higher self. Green sapphire sparks wisdom. Orange sapphire spurs creativity. Yellow sapphire encourages prosperity.

ORIGIN

Australia, Brazil,
Czech Republic, India, Kenya,
Myanmar, Sri Lanka

COLORS

Blue, green, orange, yellow

PRIMARY USES

Enhances focus, provides calming energy, assists communication with higher realms, sparks intuition, aids connection with higher self, facilitates connection with the Divine

CHAKRA

All chakras, depending on color

PLACEMENT

Place on or touching any chakra, carry yellow sapphire in wallet for prosperity, wear as any type of jewelry, carry in a pocket, hold in both hands

Sardonyx

Sardonyx is a banded variety of chalcedony (a type of quartz), with alternating layers of sard and onyx. Most common by far is red or brown with swirls of black or white. You can also find sardonyx in blue with black swirls, although that is the more rare combination. The stone tends to be deeply colored and opaque.

ORIGIN

Brazil, India, Japan, Turkey, United States

COLORS

Red, red-orange, brown, blue

PRIMARY USES

Increases mental focus, promotes optimism, provides protection, stabilizes relationships, attracts luck, imparts mental discipline

CHAKRA

Root, sacral

PLACEMENT

Place on or touching the appropriate chakras, carry in pants pocket, tape to the bottom of an office or study chair

Selenite

Selenite is a very high-vibration stone. It is milky white with white striations or ridges. A variety of gypsum, it has a soft texture, so you need to be very careful because it damages easily. You can find selenite as rough or smooth stones, and you can also find it in carvings. Some people use selenite towers on lighted bases, and the selenite glows with the changing colors of the light. Don't use water or salt to cleanse this crystal.

ORIGIN

France, Germany, Great Britain, Greece, Mexico, Poland, Russia, United States

COLORS

White

PRIMARY USES

Promotes communication with higher self and the Divine, sparks inspiration, cleanses and purifies energy, cleanses other crystals, fosters enlightenment, provides protective energy

CHAKRA

Crown

PLACEMENT

Place on or touching the crown chakra, carry in a pocket, hold in either hand, place around an area for psychic protection or energy cleansing, keep in meditation space

Sodalite

Sodalite displays as a denim blue color with white or black striations and spots. It looks a little like lapis lazuli, but the coloring is lighter.

ORIGIN

Brazil, Canada, France, Greenland, Myanmar, Romania, Russia, United States

COLORS

Blue

PRIMARY USES

Promotes truth and integrity, enables better communication (particularly in communications fields such as writing), increases intuition, promotes psychic abilities

CHAKRA

Throat, third eye

PLACEMENT

Place on or touching the appropriate chakras, hold in the receiving (nondominant) hand, wear as a necklace or earrings, keep in the office to spark creativity

Spinel

Sparkling crystalline gemstones, spinel comes in many colors, although the most common is red. The stones tend to be quite small, and they are clear but often contain inclusions within the crystals.

ORIGIN

Canada, India, Pakistan, Sri Lanka

COLORS

Pink, red

PRIMARY USES

Sparks renewal, encourages love, provides encouragement during difficult times, helps ease emotions during a crisis or following a trauma

CHAKRA

Root, heart

PLACEMENT

Place on or touching the appropriate chakras, carry in a pocket, wear as jewelry of any kind, hold in either hand, carry in pants pocket during difficult times

Sugilite

Pronounced "*sooj*-a-lite," this purple opaque stone has banding of contrasting color, white to brown, running through it. The stone is lightly sparkly. It is also called lavulite. It is a relatively rare stone.

ORIGIN

Japan, South Africa

COLORS

Light purple, pinkish purple, violet

PRIMARY USES

Helps ease feelings of loneliness, supports meditation, facilitates connection with spirit, aids in making life decisions, helps with forgiveness and self-acceptance, banishes nightmares, facilitates connection with higher self, increases psychic awareness, strengthens healing abilities

CHAKRA

Third eye, crown

PLACEMENT

Place on or touching the appropriate chakras, keep in meditation area, place under a pillow or on a bedside table, wear as a necklace or earrings, carry in a pocket, hold in either hand

Sulfur

Sulfur is a beautiful and bright yellow stone. Opaque and irregular, with sparkling bits of crystal on the surface and throughout, the stone detoxifies and absorbs negativity. Pure elemental sulfur, used in everything from fertilizer to medicine to matches, is not toxic. However, the physical crystal can be reactive with other elements. Do not leave it near a heater or lamp where it can release gases. Never use water or salt to cleanse this crystal.

ORIGIN

Anywhere near volcanoes

COLORS

Bright yellow

PRIMARY USES

Helps people overcome feelings of negativity, increases connection with inner feelings and motivations, removes emotional barriers, fosters self-esteem

CHAKRA

Solar plexus

PLACEMENT

Place on the solar plexus chakra, hold in either hand, place in work area or other frequented area to enhance self-worth (wash hands after touching)

Sunstone

Sunstone is a pretty orange to yellow-orange stone that is lightly translucent with small sparkly pieces in it. It is a form of feldspar, and it can be very clear or it might be milky or opaque, depending on the piece.

ORIGIN

Canada, Greece, India, Norway, United States

COLORS

Yellow-orange to orange or peach

PRIMARY USES

Promotes positive energy, enhances optimism, helps change negative thoughts to positive thoughts, strengthens affirmations, fosters self-worth

CHAKRA

Sacral, solar plexus

PLACEMENT

Place on or touching the appropriate chakras, hold in either hand, carry in a pocket, wear as jewelry (particularly bracelets and rings), keep in meditation area

Super Seven

Also known as melody stone, sacred seven or super 7, this is a high-vibration stone. It is a stone that naturally contains seven different types of quartz: clear quartz, amethyst, smoky quartz, cacoxenite, rutile, geothite, and lepidocroncite. It tends to look like a piece of amethyst with major areas of different materials throughout, and its appearance will vary greatly depending on the composition. Super seven has a very strong vibrational feeling in the hand, almost to the point of discomfort if you hold it too long, because it has such a powerful energy.

ORIGIN

All around the world

COLORS

Purple with gray, black, clear, and brown

PRIMARY USES

Strengthens connection to the Divine and higher realms, awakens psychic insight, integrates all the chakras, helps in the discovery of life's path, amplifies energy

CHAKRA

All chakras

PLACEMENT

Place on crown chakra and below root chakra to cleanse and energize chakras, place on third eye or crown chakra, hold in the receiving (nondominant) hand, keep in meditation area

Tanzanite

A beautiful blue to violet stone, tanzanite is clear, and when cut into faceted gemstones makes beautiful jewelry. It is a form of the mineral zoisite, and it gets its name from its origins in Tanzania. It is a relatively rare stone.

ORIGIN

Tanzania

COLORS

Blue to violet

PRIMARY USES

Enhances communications with spirit, fosters psychic abilities, facilitates exploration of spirituality, raises consciousness, soothes and calms

CHAKRA

Third eye, crown

PLACEMENT

Place on the appropriate chakras, wear as jewelry (particularly necklace or earrings), carry in a pocket, keep in meditation area, place near bed to aid in spiritual development during sleep

Tigers Eye

Blue is one of the three main colors of tigers eye. The other two are red and yellow. You can sometimes find all of the colors in a single stone, or you can find them in stones by themselves. Blue tigers eye has a deep gray blue color (sometimes so dark it's almost black, especially when it's unpolished) with darker gray bands running through it, and the stone has an iridescent sheen. It is a moderately hard stone.

ORIGIN

Australia, Canada, India, Mexico, South Africa, United States

COLORS

Deep blue-gray with darker gray bands

PRIMARY USES

Induces calmness, reduces stress, facilitates clear communication, provides insight, balances yin and yang, improves intuition and psychic abilities

CHAKRA

Third eye, throat

PLACEMENT

Place on or touching the appropriate chakras, wear around the neck as jewelry or an amulet, carry in a pocket, hold in either hand, place anywhere better communication is needed, place in meditation area, place anywhere energy feels imbalanced

Tigers Eye

Red tigers eye is a banded stone that has a reddish cast with darker red or brown striations. Even unpolished, it has a sheen to it, and the polished form has a metallic luminescence.

ORIGIN

Australia, Canada, India, Mexico, South Africa, United States

COLORS

Red, mahogany, brown

PRIMARY USES

Stimulates sex drive, enhances motivation and willpower, promotes action, boosts confidence, provides energy and protection

CHAKRA

Root

PLACEMENT

Place on or touching the root chakra, hold in the receiving (nondominant) hand, tape to the bottom of a desk chair to spur the motivation to work, place under the mattress for sexual energy, carry in pants pocket for willpower

YELLOW

Tigers Eye

Yellow tigers eye is a brown and yellow stone with stripes of each of the colors running through it. Although the stone is opaque, it has a beautiful sparkle that gives it the quality of a cat's eye—hence its name.

ORIGIN

Australia, Canada, India, Mexico, South Africa, United States

COLORS

Yellow/gold, brown

PRIMARY USES

Enhances personal power, strengthens sense of self, boosts self-confidence and self-esteem, aids in decision-making, breaks cycles of inaction, increases courage

CHAKRA

Solar plexus

PLACEMENT

Place on or touching your solar plexus chakra, wear as a bracelet or ring, carry in a pants or shirt pocket, hold in the receiving (nondominant) hand, keep in meditation area

Topaz

Topaz is a transparent blue or yellow gemstone frequently cut into facets and used in jewelry. In its cut and polished form, it is very clear. It is a precious gemstone, and the cut pieces tend to be fairly small. Blue topaz enhances communication and increases connection to higher realms. Yellow topaz boosts self-esteem and helps with setting boundaries.

ORIGIN

Africa, Australia, India, Mexico, Pakistan, United States

COLORS

Blue or yellow

PRIMARY USES

Fosters forgiveness, enhances truth and integrity, assists with clear communication, helps tune in to thoughts, recharges energy, increases empathy, attracts abundance, fosters joy

CHAKRA

Third eye, throat (blue), solar plexus (yellow)

PLACEMENT

Place on or touching the appropriate chakras, wear as any type of jewelry, put yellow variety in a wallet or cash box to attract abundance, keep blue topaz in meditation area

Tourmaline

Tourmaline is a precious gemstone prized for its clear and beautiful color. Black is one of the many colors of tourmaline, and it is very commonly used in metaphysical and spiritual practice for protection from negative energy. Black tourmaline is also known as schorl. Because it absorbs so much energy, it's important to cleanse black tourmaline regularly.

ORIGIN

Afghanistan, Australia, Brazil, Mozambique, Sri Lanka, Tanzania, United States

COLORS

Black

PRIMARY USES

Absorbs negative energy, transforms negative energy to positive energy, supports grounding, offers psychic protection, provides energetic protection, helps with stress release

CHAKRA

Root

PLACEMENT

Place on or touching the root chakra, hold in either hand, carry in a pocket, wear as an amulet, use as a wedge with a negative person, keep on the desk or in the car to absorb negative energy, carry to highly charged psychic atmospheres, keep next to the bed to absorb negative energy during sleep

GREEN

Tourmaline

Green tourmaline has a lovely green color and is commonly used as a precious gemstone in jewelry. Along with the polished and cut stones, you can find rough green tourmaline, which may be in polished stones or points with a clear green color. It is also known as verdelite.

ORIGIN

Afghanistan, Australia, Brazil, Mozambique, Sri Lanka, Tanzania, United States

COLORS

Green

PRIMARY USES

Aids heart healing (emotional and physical), promotes luck, increases prosperity, amplifies physical and emotional energy and endurance, enhances gardening abilities

CHAKRA

Heart

PLACEMENT

Place on the heart chakra, wear as jewelry (particularly a necklace or bracelet), hold in the receiving (nondominant) hand, carry in a pocket, keep in a garden shed or with plants, keep in wallet or cashbox

PINK

Tourmaline

Pink tourmaline is a clear pink gemstone. It is often polished and used in jewelry, and is fairly expensive. It is a high-vibration stone. You can find the stones by themselves or as bands of tourmaline embedded in other stones.

ORIGIN

Afghanistan, Australia, Brazil, Mozambique, Sri Lanka, Tanzania, United States

COLORS

Pink

PRIMARY USES

Promotes joy, promotes universal love, spurs romantic love, enhances positive emotions

CHAKRA

Heart

PLACEMENT

Place on or touching the heart chakra, wear as jewelry (particularly a necklace or bracelet), hold in either hand, carry to promote universal love, wear on romantic dates, place on bedside table or under pillow to promote positivity during sleep

WATERMELON

Tourmaline

Watermelon tourmaline gets its name because it resembles a slice of watermelon. It has green, white, and pink shades throughout. The gemstone is very clear and banded, and it is often cut into jewelry. It is a fairly expensive gemstone.

ORIGIN

Afghanistan, Australia, Brazil, Mozambique, Sri Lanka, Tanzania, United States

COLORS

Pink, green, white

PRIMARY USES

Promotes all types of love, balances energies, inspires creativity, allows connection with nature, balances chakras, heals emotional pain, promotes peace and calmness

CHAKRA

Heart

PLACEMENT

Place on or touching the heart chakra, wear as jewelry of any kind, carry in a pocket, hold in either hand, keep in a creative workspace, carry or wear when out in nature

Turquoise

An opaque stone, turquoise comes in shades of blue to turquoise with dark or light veins running through. Turquoise is very popular in jewelry, especially that associated with the American Southwest. Many manufacturers dye howlite to look like turquoise (sometimes called howlite turquoise), so it's important to be sure you're working with the actual stone.

ORIGIN

All around the world

COLORS

Blue, turquoise

PRIMARY USES

Serves as a bridge between the spiritual and the physical, facilitates connection to the universe, allows for honest and truthful communication, helps with free expression, provides strength, provides protection, purifies energy

CHAKRA

Throat, third eye

PLACEMENT

Place on or touching the appropriate chakras, keep in meditation area, wear as any type of jewelry, carry in a pocket, hold in either hand

Unakite

Unakite is mossy green with peach to pink large spots and flecks of gold throughout. It is a form of jasper. You may find it in rough stones or tumbled and polished.

ORIGIN

South Africa, United States

COLORS

Mossy green with pink/peach and flecks of darker green and gold

PRIMARY USES

Promotes emotional balance, improves sleep, fights addiction, increases willpower

CHAKRA

Solar plexus, heart

PLACEMENT

Place on or touching the appropriate chakras, place under pillow or on bedside table, hold in either hand, carry in a pocket

Vanadinite

Vanadinite is formed naturally when a mineral ore that contains lead becomes oxidized. This stone is yellow to orange to red, and has clear crystals in boxy clusters. The brightly colored crystals are transparent and quite small.

ORIGIN

Morocco, United States

COLORS

Yellow, orange, red

PRIMARY USES

Boosts creativity and motivation, provides mental stimulation, energizes, spurs action

CHAKRA

Sacral

PLACEMENT

Place directly on the sacral chakra, tape to the bottom of a chair or place on the desk of a creative workspace, place under mattress or pillow or on bed-side table to awake refreshed and energized

Zircon

This semiprecious gemstone comes in blue, yellow, red, brown, or clear. Many people confuse it with cubic zirconium, but they aren't the same. Zircon is a naturally occurring mineral with metaphysical properties, while cubic zirconia is a synthetic material with no metaphysical properties.

ORIGIN

Australia, Cambodia, Canada, Middle East, Myanmar, Sri Lanka, Tanzania

COLORS

Yellow, blue (other colors are likely heat treated)

PRIMARY USES

Enhances self-love, supports spiritual growth, enhances communication with higher self, amplifies spiritual and Divine energy, aids intuition

CHAKRA

Crown, third eye, throat

PLACEMENT

Place on or touching the appropriate chakras, keep in meditation area, wear as jewelry (particularly necklace or earrings), carry in a shirt pocket

Zoisite

Many gemstones, such as tanzanite and thulite, are forms of zoisite, but here we refer to green zoisite. The color ranges from light to dark green, and it may be found naturally with ruby in it, much like fuchsite. Zoisite has little sparkling bits throughout the rock, and it is an opaque stone.

ORIGIN

Austria, Cambodia, India, Kenya, Madagascar, Russia, Sri Lanka, Tanzania

COLORS

Green

PRIMARY USES

Opens the heart, strengthens love relationships, spurs action, combats laziness

CHAKRA

Heart

PLACEMENT

Place on or touching the heart chakra, wear as a necklace, carry in a shirt pocket, hold in either hand

Glossary

AFFIRMATION A positive statement you make as a form of meditation about something you'd like to see in your life. The statement is made as if the goal has already been achieved. For example, "I am healthy, happy, and prosperous." Also see *mantra*.

AURA Part of the energetic anatomy; the spiritual energy that surrounds the body, holding energetic information about a person as an emotional being, physical being, and spiritual being.

CHAKRA An energetic vortex in the body. The seven main chakras (see illustration on page 23) have specific colors and physical, energetic, and spiritual properties associated with them.

CHARGING A method of imparting energy into crystals so that they will function at their highest vibrational level when you use them, usually done after cleansing or with new crystals.

CLEANSING A method of clearing accumulated energy from crystals, usually done with saltwater, energetic intention, or holding in a stream of smoke (smudging).

DIVINE Another word for God, Source, higher consciousness, or any innate intelligence one believes exists in the universe.

ENERGY, PSYCHIC Any type of energy not currently measurable by scientific instruments, including intuition, extra-sensory perception (ESP), clairvoyance, psychokinesis, and healing.

ENERGY WORK/ENERGY HEALING Working with spiritual energy to bring about physical, spiritual, emotional, or mental change or healing. Crystal healing is a form of energy healing.

GROUNDING A way for an individual to connect to the Earth for the purpose of maintaining balance among his/her physical, mental, emotional, and spiritual aspects.

HAND, GIVING In energy work, this is the hand that shares energy and healing with others. This is the dominant hand, generally the one a person writes with.

HAND, RECEIVING In healing work, this is the hand through which energy is received. This is the nondominant hand, generally the one a person does not write with.

HIGHER CONSCIOUSNESS
The consciousness of one's higher self, in which one can access the Divine, universal consciousness from which all things derive. Meditation is one method by which people seek to attain higher consciousness.

HIGHER SELF The part of an individual that is in touch with his/her spirit's path, enabling that person to access higher consciousness; other terms may include higher spirit or soul.

INTUITION Information received from a source of higher consciousness or higher self by way of the third eye chakra.

LAW OF ATTRACTION A spiritual principle stating that people attract from the universe what they think, say, do, and point their energy toward, for positive or negative.

LIFE FORCE The divine energy, such as prana or Chi, that animates all living beings.

MANTRA In this book, an affirmative statement that focuses on a positive desired outcome or state of being, or an acknowledgment and gratitude for what is.

MANTRA MEDITATION A form of meditation in which the practitioner sits quietly and chants a mantra (aloud or to oneself) to keep the mind focused and to create positive energy.

MERIDIAN An energetic pathway running through the body. The human body has 12 meridians, each associated with different organs.

MINDFULNESS MEDITATION A form of meditation in which the practitioner sits quietly and allows thoughts to arise, noticing them as they do and then releasing them fully.

MOVEMENT MEDITATION A form of meditation in which the practitioner performs repetitive movements, such as walking slowly, to keep the mind focused and clear.

NUMEROLOGY A branch of knowledge dealing with the metaphysical significance of numbers.

PATH Your path—referred to variously in this book as your spirit's path, life's path, and soul's path— is the path you follow on this Earth, which includes the lessons you need to learn, the karma you attempt to balance through your actions and reactions, and the people you need to meet, among other things.

PRESENT The moment of now; keeping one's attention on the now (present-time focus) relieves worries about the past and the future and increases gratitude and appreciation.

PROGRAMMING A method of imparting energy and intention into crystals, usually through meditation or energy transfer, so that crystal will perform for the intended purpose. This is usually performed after cleansing and charging.

PROSPERITY CORNER A feng shui concept, this is an area of the home that attracts abundance and prosperity. The prosperity corner is located in the farthest back left corner of the home when facing inward.

REIKI A form of energy healing that calls upon universal energy to impart healing, either through the hands or through the mental application of energy.

SHAMAN, SHAMANIC WORK A person who is able to work with spirits and the spiritual. Shamanic work involves working with spirits to eliminate negativity and increase positive energy/spirits.

SPIRIT GUIDE A being of higher consciousness that exists to help you along your path, often appearing through dreams, inspiration, and intuition.

UNCONDITIONAL LOVE Pure spiritual love that exists without conditions of any kind, regardless of the behavior or actions of others.

VISUALIZATION A meditative act in which the practitioner creates mental images, or pictures, with the intention of manifesting the experience in reality.

WORRY STONE A smooth, flat stone that is rubbed with the thumb to relieve stress or tension or to impart the energy from the stone to you.

Resources

CRYSTAL-CURE.COM
A commercial website with a range of crystals and products, as well as information on using crystals and their properties.

ETSY.COM
A commerce website with a range of crystals, crystal beads, and jewelry available from individual sellers.

HEALINGCRYSTALS.COM
A commercial website with a range of crystals and products, as well as wonderful articles about crystals. Knowledgeable and helpful, the people who run this website suggest crystal healing solutions and answer questions about crystals.

HEALING-CRYSTALS-FOR-YOU.COM
An informational website that offers comprehensive information about crystals, including A-to-Z listings of crystals along with their healing and metaphysical properties.

MYSS.COM
The official website of author and medical intuitive Caroline Myss. Included on this website under Free Resources is a detailed flash animation called *Chakras: Your Energetic Being,* which outlines the chakra system and the issues associated with each chakra.

Along with the books listed in the References section (see page 350), consider the following.

THE CHAKRA BIBLE
by Patricia Mercier (Sterling, 2007)
Discusses the chakras, attuning them, how they work, and so on.

CRYSTAL HEALING
by Judy Hall (Godsfield, 2010)
Provides crystal healing prescriptions and meditations for healing.

CRYSTAL THERAPY
by Doreen Virtue, PhD, and Judith Lukomski (Hay House, 2005)
Provides information about crystal healing.

THE REIKI BIBLE
by Eleanor McKenzie (Sterling, 2009)
Covers the basics of Reiki energy healing techniques.

THE SUBTLE BODY
by Cyndi Dale (Sounds True, 2009)
An encyclopedia of energy anatomy, covering chakras, auras, meridians, and how people's energy anatomy interacts with their physical body.

References

BOOKS

Gauding, Madonna. *The Meditation Bible: The Definitive Guide to Meditations for Every Purpose.* New York: Sterling, 2005.

Hall, Judy. *The Crystal Bible.* Blue Ash, OH: Walking Stick Press, 2003.

Hall, Judy. *Crystal Prescriptions: The A–Z Guide to Over 1,200 Symptoms and Their Healing Crystals.* Poole, UK: John Hunt Publishing, 2014.

Hall, Judy. *The Encyclopedia of Crystals.* Gloucester, MA: Fair Winds Press, 2013.

Myss, Caroline. *Anatomy of the Spirit: The Seven Stages of Power and Healing.* New York: Harmony, 1996.

Myss, Caroline. *Why People Don't Heal and How They Can.* New York: Harmony, 1998.

Permutt, Philip. *The Crystal Healer: Crystal Prescriptions That Will Change Your Life Forever.* London: CICO Books, 2007.

Simmons, Robert. *Stones of the New Consciousness: Healing, Awakening, and Co-creating with Crystals, Minerals, and Gems.* Berkeley, CA: North Atlantic Books, 2009.

Tolle, Eckhart. *The Power of Now: A Guide to Spiritual Enlightenment.* Novato, CA: New World Library, 1999.

Zuckerman, Desda. *Your Sacred Anatomy: An Owner's Guide to the Human Energy Structure.* Novato, CA: Spirit Way Press, 2012.

WEBSITES

Encyclopedia Britannica. "Einstein's Mass-Energy Relation: Physics." Accessed July 21, 2015. www.britannica.com/science /Einsteins-mass-energy-relation.

International Gem Society (IGS). "What Is a Crystal?" Accessed July 21, 2015. www.gemsociety.org /article/crystal/.

The Kabbalah Centre. "The Zohar for Healing." Accessed August 20, 2015. www.zohar.com/article/zohar-healing.

McCartney, Francesca. "The Academy Journal: A Brief History of Energy Medicine." Academy of Intuition Medicine. Accessed July 21, 2015. www.intuitionmedicine.com/academy /journalarticles/journal2.htm.

McLeod, Saul. "Maslow's Hierarchy of Needs." Simply Psychology. September 17, 2007, updated 2014. Accessed July 21, 2015. www.simplypsychology.org /maslow.html.

Wisdom Library. "Seven Factors of Enlightenment." Accessed August 20, 2015. www.wisdomlib.org/definition /seven-factors-of-enlightenment /index.html.

SACRED TEXTS

The Bible: New International Version. London: Hodder & Stoughton, 2007.

The Holy Bible: English Standard Version. Wheaton, IL: Crossway Bibles, 2011.

The Koran. Translated by N. J. Dawood. New York: Penguin Classics, 2015.

Yajur Veda: Authentic English Translation. Translated by Dr. Tulsi Ram. New Delhi, India: Agniveer, 2013.

Index

Acknowledgments

I've been very blessed to have wonderfully supportive mentors, friends, and loved ones in my life as I've moved forward on my metaphysical and spiritual journey. I'd like to thank the following people: Jim Frazier, Tanner Koenen, Kevin Frazier, Patty Valdez, Howard Batie, Michaela Rand, Ashley Barrett, Cheryl Knight, Chad Wilson, Chuck Gotski, the entire South Sound Paranormal Research team, Stacy Wagner-Kinnear, and the many other wonderful friends, teachers, editors, peers, and souls whom I have encountered.

About the Author

KAREN FRAZIER is an ordained metaphysical minister, intuitive energy healer, and Usui Reiki practitioner. She holds bachelor's and master's degrees in metaphysical science and a PhD in metaphysical parapsychology. She writes a metaphysics and energy healing column and a dream interpretation column for *Paranormal Underground Magazine*.

CPSIA information can be obtained at www.ICGtesting.com
Printed in the USA
BVOW05s0324070916

461179BV00010B/10/P

9 781623 156756